CURRENCY
in an Independent Scotland

compiled by

Andy Anderson

First edition published March 2016.

Author Andy Anderson

Acknowledgements:

My thanks are due to many people for assistance and advice in preparing this wee book. I can't of course list everyone who has helped me but I must thank Ronnie Morrison, Alistair Mackinnon, Shaun Anderson, Theresa Derbyshire, Margaret Doig, Hamish Kirk, Ruth McManus and Chic McClair of Airdrie Print. For the errors that remain they are all my responsibility.

Published by Andy Anderson, 17, Broomfield Drive, Dunoon PA23 7LJ.

Printed and Bound by Airdrie Print Services Ltd., 24-26, Flowerhill Street, Airdrie, North Lanarkshire. ML6 6BH.

ISBN 978-0-992828401-7

Front Cover: The background picture is of the New Queensferry Crossing under construction. The bridge is 2,700 metres, or 1.7 miles long and is the longest in the world of this type of design. The bridge is scheduled to open this year on time and within its £1.3 billion budget.

Contents

Introduction

Democracy 5
Currency & the economy 7
Clearing away the fog 8
Money or Wealth 10
Political Independence 11
Second Option 12
Banking reform in Scotland................................ 13

Chapter 1

Inter-Government Agreement 15
You can't have our pound.................................. 18
Lifting the fog.. 20
The financial elite 23
Exposing part of the iceberg.............................. 26
An agreement which disadvantages none.......... 29

Chapter 2

Sharing UK debt... 31
Moral Obligation 31
Economic Sense... 34
Scottish Power... 36
The Wider Market 39
Scotland r-UK agreement................................... 41
Scottish Public Investment................................. 43
UK Government Decision.................................... 45

Chapter 3

Option 2.. 47
What is wrong with Sterling?............................. 48
Does Sterling cause economic problems?.......... 55
Currency Changes 57
Full Reserve Currency 59

Chapter 4

Economic development.. 67
Domestic Currency 72
Banking Reform – Merchant Banks 75
Savings and Investment..................................... 77
Scottish Government Preparations 78

Chapter 5

International Comparisons.................................. 85
Iceland.. 87
Panama 91
Greece 93
Further International comparisons..................... 97
Lessons to be drawn.. 99
Domestic Currency 101
Scotland's Currency.. 104
The Scottish pound 106

Chapter 6

Scottish Sovereignty 109
Land and Territorial rights 113
Defending Land... 115
Constitutional Currency.................................... 117
Written Constitution.. 119
The way forward.. 121
Why are we supporting Scottish Independence 123

Chapter 7

Value of Money – Revision 127
Philosophy.. 130
Financial Capitalism 134
Media Influence.. 137
Postal Ballot Rigging 141
Reasons for an Independence Referendum 144

Foreword

The foreword in this book is somewhat different from the usual style of foreword. It is not written by a celebrity who sings the praises of the author and the work. It is written by someone who read and studied the book written by Ronnie Morrison and I 'Moving On' and who found that book helpful. Hamish Kirk, who writes this forward was a teacher by profession but had, as he says, tried to avoid economics and finance before he came across our wee book. I am delighted that Hamish found our book helpful and I'm sure he will find this book equally helpful in showing a way forward through the fog of deception which surrounds these important issues.

Andy Anderson

In the summer of 2014, together with many others in Scotland and beyond, I was involved in campaigning for the Yes Vote in the Scottish Referendum. It was during those heady days that I first came across Andy Anderson and the book 'Moving On' written by Andy and by Ronnie Morrison. The Bute office of the Yes Campaign was distributing copies and one found its way onto my desk. At college and in adult life I had always avoided Economics as an academic subject and as a political topic, "Too hard" was my thought, particularly when I recalled the frightening textbooks like Samuelson's 'Economics' that I had seen in the past.

The question of the currency kept on surfacing in the debates in and around the referendum and I decided to tackle Andy & Ronnie's book on this tough subject. I found it readable and thought it deserved a wider audience. Andy kindly agreed to come to Rothesay to lead a series of discussion sessions on Economic, Political Economy and the way forward.

We met in the fine modernist surroundings of the Pavilion in Rothesay. This was before it was closed for renovation, and like the British economy the building where we held the sessions was in a bad way. I was however greatly encouraged by the turnout, which started high and remained high until the last session so people enjoyed taking part. The level of the discussions were high people seemed to be energised by the campaign and were seeking more knowledge. Seemingly simple questions like "What is money?" and "Where does credit come from?" we began to realise were not metaphysical but relate to the real world in which we live, work and eat.

Participants came to the group after a busy day and grappled with questions like "What is this Quantitative Easing?" and "What was Bretton Woods all about?" We discovered that simple questions don't always have simple answers and frequently not the answers we expected, but we persevered.

To my surprise I learned what PFI was and what an enormous confidence trick was pulled on us all through the modern banking system. Andy illustrated some of the trickery by looking at the Skye Bridge financial story – which was the theme of an earlier book he had written.

The referendum ended in defeat and we are now in a new phase of political and historical development. The mainstream media is obsessed with the EU referendum, but still provides no real analysis of what is going on. We are encouraged to obsess with celebrities and fashions, with trivia. I will read Andy's new book 'Currency – In an Independent Scotland' with interest and would recommend it to those who are interested in how our society works. It is by studying the society we live in that we can learn how to change and improve it.

Hamish Kirk

Rothesay February 2016.

Currency – In an Independent Scotland

Introduction.

In sitting down to write this book, I am making a second attempt to bring this important issue to the attention of the public hopefully with more success this time.

In February 2014, Ronnie Morrison and I published a wee book called 'Moving On' which looked at the economic and financial reasons why an independent Scotland, which we strongly support, should have its own currency in order to secure the full economic potential for the Scottish people.

We felt at that time that this issue needed to be effectively addressed if the Yes Campaign were to win the independence referendum. Well, it was not properly addressed and we now know the consequences.

Democracy

We failed to win a sufficient number of our fellow Scots to support independence. I am not among those who claim that there was a democratic decision against independence in that ballot. Primarily, because the process carried out was not 'democratic'. Democracy requires an even playing field for each side, and in the important area of information and media this was clearly not the case, with even the 'neutral' BBC playing for the No team. Also there is the sound case produced by the Democratic Socialist Federation in their report 'Defending Democracy' which demonstrates that the Postal Ballot, which is wide open to abuse, was rigged, probably by MI5 in the referendum. If you doubt this, I recommend you look at their report.*

Many people find it hard to accept that David Cameron would have authorised MI5 to get involved in rigging the Independence Referendum Ballot. History suggests otherwise. We only have to look at the bitter divisions created in Irish Society over the question of Irish Independence to know that the British Establishment will stop at nothing to keep control of any part of these Islands. Indeed we now know that MI5 with the RUC and British Army Intelligence, employed death squads, 'assassins' in a conflict which cost 3,600 lives and 40,000 injuries. If UK Governments would do this, which they have now admitted, in order to hold onto Ireland, then rigging a ballot to hold Scotland is nothing by comparison.

However, irrespective of this, Scotland will achieve our independence, and will do so without bitter internal conflict in the same way as we achieved 'devolution'. Those of us who believed in it put the case effectively and persistently until we won over the great majority of the Scottish people to the cause.

Remember our first vote on devolution failed, not that we lost the vote, indeed numerically we won, in that a majority of voters voted for devolution; But Westminster decided that by its rules we had lost. The fact that there was division and miss-representation, and even a promised 'vow' from the Tories did not help, but the main issue then, as now, is that we did not persuade enough Scots to want this and press for it. There is no doubt that if we had a vote on devolution today the unionists would struggle to get 10% of the Scottish vote.

We did not do enough to win a clear majority of the people in 1979 on the devolution issue, it is true that the terms of the voting was rigged and the media and establishment undermined our efforts; But we learned from that experience and in 1997 we won clear majorities on each of the two questions in the devolution referendum.

Irrespective of the circumstances of the Independence Referendum in 2014, if we learn the lessons and continue to build our case we will win the next referendum on Scottish Independence and that might not be all that far away.

What is without doubt now is that 'the genie is out of the bottle' in the independence campaign and it will not go back in. The issue of Scottish independence is now a significant aspect of Scottish politics and most Scots know that we will have to set-up another referendum on this issue in the relatively near future. What many of us recognise is that we must not repeat the same mistakes that were made last time.

Currency & the economy

As we suspected, one of the big mistakes, indeed according to one influential poll* by far the biggest mistake, was the currency issue. This issue alone lost the referendum for us, but of course it was a link to other issues like savings and pensions which played into the hands of the 'project fear' merchants and their media army.

So once again I have decided to write about this issue and to address not only why I believe that the currency issue is central to Scotland's economic future, but to address the important political question of how we should approach this issue before the next independence campaign begins and how we take this complex issue out of the fog of obscurity which makes it difficult for most voters to penetrate and which makes it such a good subject for the project fear merchants.

In our book 'Moving On', we set out our views about the economic policies an independent Scotland should follow and in most respects it was not much different from the policies which the SNP Government in Scotland was advocating. Free and well provisioned public health and education services, a sound Government funded infrastructure and a viable free market economy with a Keynesian style managed public investment strategy to create and maintain full employment in a high wage economy which was high tech and sustainable.

Indeed the one big difference we had with the Scottish Government's policy was on currency. I am of the view that an independent Scotland, if it wants to achieve the above economic objectives, would need its own currency and to entirely reform the banking structure so that money supply and monetary policy were in the hands of the Scottish people, through their elected Government.

When we published our book, in the run-up to the referendum we were well aware that many Scots, like us, did not support what was then the SNP Government's policy of an independent Scotland staying within Sterling with the existing banking structure; we were however constrained by the imminence of the referendum and did not want to have an open challenge to the SNP during that campaign.

This however is a different situation. We feel that this question of what currency an independent Scotland should use is one which must now be addressed, before we get into another pre-referendum debate. There are many genuine differences of opinion on this issue in Scotland and ultimately this issue must be settled by a vote, in an independent Scottish Parliament, where the Scottish people through their elected representatives can make a sovereign decision. However in the meantime we need to have a clear position in the referendum debate, which is well understood by the voters and which preserves the final decision for the Scottish people after independence.

Is it possible to find such a clear policy position which keeps people's final options open, yet gives the Yes Campaign a policy they can unite around in the referendum debate? I believe there is and I hope in this wee book to convince many yes supporters throughout Scotland that there is.

Clearing away the fog

In presenting my case for this political strategy I want to also explain and present the basis of my economic and financial strategy in a way which clears away much of the 'fog' which obscures this subject in the established media, so that the many thousands who have become politically active in Scotland can get a better vision of the economic factors which are so important to our lives.

In doing this I will examine the 'real' issues around "sharing the pound" and hitching our wagon to the present banking system. You will find things in this book which you will not find in the media, or in many academic books. I will however endeavour to ensure that what I claim is a true and accurate description of the issues I am addressing even if it is from an unusual angle.

I will give some international examples of other small countries with different types of relationship between the currency they use and their domestic economy; in order to illustrate the significance of the link between a Government's power over the currency and its ability to carry through its economic policy.

Since the book, 'Moving On' was published we have all had the opportunity to observe not only what happened in the referendum campaign in Scotland and the role played by 'currency' in that campaign, but also what happened in a politically independent Greece attempting to oppose 'austerity' with again 'currency' playing a central part.

We need to consider both these experiences, in their context, and draw lessons from them which we know of course is the best way to advance human knowledge. I will try to help with that in this book.

We all remember the media campaign over the 'pound' in the final stage of the independence campaign. To some of us, who have an understanding of the role of money in the economy, the whole thing appeared like some childish playground game. You know the sort, "it's my ball and if I don't get to be goalie, I'm taking my ball away". With others responding with the assertion "no you won't take the ball away we know you are only kidding."

The currency issue was addressed in the same childish way. With the No Campaign, backed by the UK Government, and unconstitutionally, by civil servants telling us "It's our pound and if you vote for independence you can't get to share it" with the Scottish Government response being "they are just bluffing" It seems all very immature and laughable, but it was not that at all. It was a dangerous, undemocratic exercise on behalf of the UK Government designed to instil fear and concern among the Scottish people, particularly the elderly and vulnerable.

Fear, feeds and develops best in ignorance. We fear most, what we understand least. So the best antidote to 'project fear', is 'project enlightenment'. The more that older people in Scotland know about the role of money or 'currency' in the economy the less likely they are going to be afraid of its possible harm to them and their families. I intend to explain, in simple and meaningful terms the real role of money in the economy so that people can't be so easily frightened by any change to the existing arrangement.

Money or Wealth

As a simple example, money, as all economists will agree, is not wealth, it has no intrinsic 'value'. It's only economic value, is its use as an exchange mechanism. Most of us, most of the time, are so familiar with money as a medium of exchange that we tend to think of it as being wealth of itself, but it is not. It has no value if it can't be exchanged for 'real goods' which represent real wealth. This is not a difficult idea to understand, but it is an easy one to create confusion with.

To illustrate this point let us just do a little exercise exploring this: If we were shipwrecked on an uninhabited island and have to return to the sinking shipwreck to rescue things and we had the choice between a large box of newly minted 100 pound notes, or a large box of old carpentry tools; which would we select? In such circumstances, where money had no 'exchange value' we would soon recognise that money had no value for us. Wealth we would seek in finding food, water, shelter and other fundamental aspects of a comfortable life and the old carpentry tools would have value for us.

In the old stories of highway robbers they would demand "hands up, your money or your life?" What if the question was, "hands up, your money or your wealth?"

Many of us tend to think of these two terms 'money' and 'wealth' as being interchangeable, the same thing really; but they are most certainly not. Money is merely a 'medium of exchange' used to transfer wealth. It is not wealth. It has no intrinsic value at all. I know that it may seem that I am repeating myself and labouring this point. Well that's good, because it implies that the point is clear, as it needs to be, for this is a vital point.

So wealth, in a real sense is the goods and services we need to ensure that our family has access to, in order to give them a good standard of living. That is a definition of real wealth. We have seen however quite recently in Greece, that in order to secure money, in the form of bank loans, the Greek Government has been forced to give up more of the Greek people's real wealth.

Giving up real goods and services (real wealth) for an exchange medium (money) which is then exchanged for other goods and service, is fine, and is how the economy normally works. ie money plays the role of an exchange medium between the exchange of real goods and services.

However a Government giving up real wealth, in exchange for money (as a commodity) from a private bank and paying high interest, as opposed to printing its own money; is a very bad deal indeed. In economic terms it is to exchange real wealth for something which has no intrinsic value.

Political Independence

We have learned from bitter experience that the currency issue for Scotland must be addressed openly and the public must be involved in a genuine and honest debate about this issue before the independence campaign properly begins again. Because in truth the question about which currency an independent Scotland should use is different, and separate, from the question of political independence.

The referendum should be about Scotland's political independence. After a majority vote for Independence, the Scottish people and the Scottish Parliament, would need to make a number of other decisions, one of which, perhaps the most important, will be what currency we will use and how our banking system will be organised and regulated.

I believe, and explain in this book, that there should and could be a temporary agreement on the currency issue between the UK and Scottish Government before any referendum campaign on independence began next time and this is my preferred option.

My view is that this important issue must not be used to confuse the issue of political independence for Scotland, as indeed it was the last time. I take the view that the Scottish and UK Governments should agree a short term (3 year) agreement which would see an independent Scotland use sterling for a period, without being integral to the Sterling set-up while the Scottish people considered if they would stay within Sterling or set up their own currency arrangements.

We have learned from experience however, that because this is a sensible option and in the interests of both Government, it is never the less an option which the UK Government might refuse to participate in.

In view of this I do not feel that we should depend on any agreement with the UK Government. I do not think Scotland's leaders should once again be left saying "Well the UK Government says they do not agree with our proposals but they are just bluffing" So I have drawn up an alternative to my first option, which we should adopt if the UK Government refuses to co-operate. This alternative would work fine for us. But it might not work so well for the UK, but that will be a decision for them to make, not us.

If such a deal could be done, which I believe is entirely possible. Then this issue could not be used by the 'No' campaign and the media in the way it was last time. The first two chapters of this book addresses this issue and why I believe that there is a good basis for an agreed arrangement to be made between the Scottish and UK Governments on this issue, before the next referendum.

Second Option

If however such an agreement does not materialize, I look in chapter three at an alternative option for Scotland and how we could deal with that eventuality. On this occasion we must put our cards on the table before the independence campaign begins so that there is no room for ambiguity or doubt.

The UK Government has a massive national debt. None of this, not one penny of it, will an independent Scotland be legally responsible for. Our efforts to get an agreement with the UK Government is to look intelligently at the currency issue, while also addressing how we can help the r-UK with their crippling debt burden.

If the UK Government is not interested in our help then that would be unfortunate, but frankly it would be more unfortunate for them, than it would be for us. If that proves to be the case we should, however reluctantly, move onto option two which would have no provision for helping the UK with their debt problem since clearly they had rejected our offer of help.

Banking reform in Scotland

In the book 'Moving On' we explained why it was important that an independent Scotland dramatically reformed the banking system and established our own 'full reserve' currency to serve the new Scottish economy. The other chapters of this wee book will look at how work on this could precede, post independence, even during a period when a 'temporary' sterling agreement was in operation.

It is well known and widely understood that the current banking system in the Western World has failed and needs drastic reform. The Turkish American economist Yalman Onaran in his book 'Zombie Banks' addresses "How broken banks and debtor Nations are crippling the Global Economy" He explains in simple terms what a 'Zombie Bank'* is. It is a bank which has more liabilities than assets which in legal terms is bankrupt, therefore legally 'dead' but because of Government support, non application of the law, and phantom money (we will look at Phantom Money later in the book) such banks continue to function. They are therefore the living dead 'Zombies' in Onaran's terms. According to this definition the four largest UK banks are Zombie banks.

It is therefore vital that the problems associated with the banking system are addressed, they should have been after their major crisis in 2008, when all Governments promised to deal with this, but none of them did, with the exception of tiny Iceland who tried. I address the core of this problem in this book and set out how an independent Scotland could deal with this issue by reforming our banking system.

I am very much of the view that the economic and financial matters I am addressing in this wee book are not complex or difficult to understand and indeed can be understood by most people who give a wee bit of attention to it. The great difficulty which most people have experienced with these subjects is that powerful vested interests, with lots of political, academic and media muscle, have brought in misleading and distorting concepts designed specifically to cover the subjects in a fog of mystery. My object is to cut through that fog and to expose the plain facts, so that most people will be able to see exactly what the issues are.

I will also in the final chapter of this book turn my attention to the political phenomenon which has swept through Scotland in the last two years, perhaps best illustrated by the almost clear sweep by the SNP of all Scottish UK Parliamentary seats, 56 out of 59.

There is, in my view, a failure to seriously analysis this political earthquake, and what is worse, a tendency for some of us on the pro-independence side to put this down to our brilliant campaigning tactics. I am sure that this movement runs much deeper in our social structure than events and tactics in the last two years. Although I don't like to admit it, I very much doubt that our 'brilliant' tactics in the Indy campaign had a lot to do with it. I believe that this movement is deeper and more profound than this, and that we need to study it carefully if we want to have an independent Scotland and to have political influence within it.

I want and expect people in Scotland to decide that like most countries in the world they want political freedom to determine their own future. I hope that when they achieve this they will also work, and vote for their 'economic' independence in order to secure a safe and prosperous future for their families. If this little book can help people to do this, my objectives will have been achieved.

* Reference for DSF 'Defending Democracy' Report

* Ashcroft Poll "How Scotland voted, and why" 19th September 2014 57% No voters influenced by pound issue.

* Yalman Onaran 'Zombie Bank'

Chapter 1

Inter-Government Agreement

Is it possible to negotiate an agreement between the Scottish and the UK Government which would allow the 'currency' issue to be taken out of the independence debate and put to one side during the campaign for Scottish independence?

As a professional trade-union negotiator for many years I learned that for any two sides to come to an agreement there needs to be one important thing on offer for each of them, which they desire to obtain or do not desire to lose. Where this is so, ever the bitterest enemies will reach an agreement and honour that agreement in order to obtain their objective.

The most difficult aspect of negotiations between parties is often where they should start from. It is true that for negotiations to succeed there needs to be an objective for each side which they want to achieve, or are keen to avoid. However, while this is a necessary condition for negotiations, it is not a sufficient one. Often it can be observed that opposing sides should sit down and try to negotiate about their differences, but seem to find it difficult, if not impossible to do so. The initial problem, which sometimes seems too difficult to overcome, is how to start negotiations. This has often led to talks about talks, in order to find common ground from which to start.

So the first thing to overcome is to find common ground which could be a basis for starting negotiations. This is very important and both sides will see how important it is to them as they accept the idea of negotiations; but of course, want to gain their objective, without conceding too much ground to their opponent. So if you ask them to concede what they see as the essence of their case before the negotiations start; then you are very unlikely to get negotiations started at all.

So where is the 'common ground' in this issue, which could lead to a basis for negotiations?

Both sides will be aware that their negotiations will take place in front of two audiences. One is the general public, who may not be particularly knowledgeable about the detail, but who do have voting power so need to be kept on-side. The other is the small ruling elite (money markets) who are well aware of the detail and will need to accept the agreement because they have considerable financial and economic power. So both sides will have to find common ground which will not seriously undermine their calculated 'relationship' with either of these audiences.

Now Cameron and Osborne have made it clear to the public audience that an independent Scotland can't 'share' the pound so any back tracking on that, before negotiations started would be seen as them having given in by this audience. The small elite audience have a different view and focus. They are interested in the UK National Debt, which is why when this matter was raised last time, they insisted that Cameron must make it clear that the UK Government would be fully responsible for the National Debt. Now they would like to see negotiations succeed, because any deal which helped the UK Government to meet its debt would suit them.

So if the Scottish Government wants the current UK Government to negotiate on the currency issue it needs to first drop its 'demand' to share the pound. It could possibly find common ground on 'using' the pound, but to ask the UK Government to go back on its publicly pronounced policy of refusing to agree that an independent Scotland could 'share' the pound would be to ask them to concede, and back down on their main point as far as their electorate was concerned, before the negotiations began. This is not likely to be acceptable to the UK Government. Negotiations are unlikely to even begin if this problem is not faced.

However, within the terms of a temporary agreement, let us say a 3 year agreement, which saw the Scottish Government use the pound sterling for external trading within a UK agreed 'special temporary arrangement' this is entirely possible, without loss of face by either side.

Now, such an agreement would not do any permanent damage to those Scots who want out of sterling, nor indeed, to those who wanted to stay permanently in the sterling area. Because, when the temporary agreement ended, an Independent Scotland would be able to decide, without outside influence, what way it wanted to go on the currency issue.

It is possible therefore that sufficient common ground could be found in this way in order to open the way for there to be fruitful negotiations, prior to a future independence referendum, between the Scottish and UK Governments. Negotiations in which both sides could see objectives well worth securing and were therefore committed to working on seriously. The negotiations themselves would be held in secret, but the outcome would be open to consideration my both audiences.

If the outcome seemed to settle the currency issue in a way which both sides were satisfied with, albeit on a temporary basis, then this particular issue would not figure greatly in the referendum campaign which followed and this would be of great value to the yes campaign, because it would prevent 'project fear' from having the same effect on this issue as it had last time.

Significantly however it would have an effect on the 'ruling elite' audience because it would offer the UK Government support to meet its National Debt obligations and this would find favour with them, and consequently with the 'money markets'.

The Scottish Government must not walk unprepared into another referendum campaign with this currency issue left open for abuse by the 'project fear' merchants and their huge media machine; while they are left with the claim "They are only bluffing". That will just not do next time.

Nor can we afford, as the Greek Government discovered, to go into a political debate entirely unprepared to have any option on currency. If we did, we would be as vulnerable as they were shown to be.

The Scottish Government, whatever its advice, or view, on currency in the new Scotland must enter the debate this time putting the 'real' cards on the table so that the 'other' audience, the ruling elite can read the cards clearly.

There is therefore a rational and sensible way forward on this issue which will offer the UK Government a long-term agreement on its National Debt problem which is acceptable to its creditors, while giving it a face-saving escape from its previous assertions that an independent Scotland could not use the pound.

The advantage to Scotland of such a deal is clear. It removes the largest 'project fear' issue from the next referendum campaign, while it retains the full range of options on currency for a future independent Scottish Parliament and people to decide.

Well it is fairly obvious why the Scottish Government should want such an agreement. This issue alone and the confusion surrounding it cost them the referendum last time. The Ashcroft Poll referred to earlier found 57% of No voters said that the currency issue was of significance to them in their vote. In addition to that many referred to pensions and savings being at risk which is related to the currency scare tactic. So if this issue could be removed from the debate with all the fear and uncertainty which it engenders then this would be a substantial gain for the 'Yes' campaign. So let us assume that the Scottish Government would be happy to make such an agreement.

Why should the UK Government be prepared to co-operate in such an agreement however?

What can the Scottish Government offer the UK Government which would make them believe that such an agreement would be in their interest? Well that may not be as difficult for them to achieve as it appears on first glance to be; but we may have to look a bit deeper to see it.

You can't have our pound

We all remember how the 'No' campaign, then the British Government, then the three Unionist political leaders, exploited the 'currency issue' for all it was worth in what they themselves called 'project fear' during the Referendum campaign.

We were told that if we voted for independence we would not be able to use the pound and that Alex Salmond had "no plan 'b' on the currency issue" Salmond had no second option they told us time and again. This claim was made and immediately repeated right across the media. It was presented simultaneously by all media outlets on its first day and for the three following days at the beginning. After the initial launch it was then regularly referred to right up to the end of the campaign. So it was clear that it was an organised planned specific campaign ploy.

Alex Salmond, who had fought a brilliant campaign, seemed unable to respond to this. He had to keep repeating that they were 'bluffing' about this and repeating that Scotland would use the pound after independence. Indeed in the TV head-to-head with Alistair Darling, which most of us expected him to dominate, he got caught again on this hook and this was seen by many voters. This damaging uncertainty and ambiguity was the main message which was driven home relentlessly by all the media. It would appear from the polls after the referendum that this issue seems to have been the most successful issue for the 'No' campaign. Indeed perhaps the only successful issue for them. Alistair Darling, who is credited with being the instigator of this media ploy, has been rewarded by David Cameron with a seat in the House of Lords.

We can all remember this vividly and for some of us the embarrassment of it. What many of us have not remembered is another formal announcement made by the UK Prime Minister, within days of the currency ploy being started. This announcement, unlike the currency issue, was short, clear and specific. It was also, directly related to the currency issue, but was not presented as such and it was of vital significance. Most people don't remember it, because it was not endlessly repeated by all the media.

The formal statement David Cameron made was that the UK Government was responsible for all the UK National Debt. He made it clear that the UK Government would retain this responsibility after the independence referendum, irrespective of the outcome. This statement was not qualified there was no mention of Scotland's 'share' of the ND. It was made clear by Cameron that all the ND was a UK responsibility.

Well let's think about that. As we previously indicated, financial issues are normally obscured by a fog of mystery, or what we called in our book 'Moving On' as "smoke and mirrors". In a sense financial policy ideas are like icebergs in the ocean. We see the surface outline but the mass of the object is not in sight and we can't see the full bulk or shape of the iceberg under the surface.

The great advantage for the No campaign of using the currency issue in its project fear propaganda was precisely this mysterious aspect of it. They felt they had Alex Salmond in a trap, and to some extent they did. They made the invalid claim that an independent Scottish Government would not be able to use the pound; then they pressed him to offer one or more alternatives.

If he started to present alternatives this would reinforce their invalid claim that his Government could not use the pound; on the other hand if he refused to be drawn down that track he could be accused of having no plan 'b'. It was the old 'Heads we win; tails you lose' trick. This was quite simple, childishly simple, trickery. It was however highly dependent on the mysteries of the financial system.

Lifting the fog

So let's see if we can clear away some of the fog and expose the working to common view.

There was, and is, no substance to the claim that an independent Scottish Government could be prevented from using sterling as its national currency. Scotland, or indeed any country, could use sterling for its internal or external use. There is nothing to prevent this, it is certainly not in the gift of Westminster politicians to extend or withhold this option. The premiss on which the challenge to Salmond was made, was itself flawed, yet it was endlessly repeated without reference to the glaring flaw at its centre.

Of course the ambiguity which existed in the public mind between using sterling and 'sharing in sterling' made it easier for the project fear merchants, and this ambiguity was Alex Salmond's fault because he should have expected them to fog the issue and he should not have left any hostages to fortune.

However the most important aspect of this iceberg which needs to be exposed relates directly to the nature of sterling. The pound sterling is a fiat currency. Which means that the "promise to pay the bearer on demand" written on the front of it no longer means that such 'payment' will be in gold or any other precious metal.

The 'promise' on the front of the pound is a promise from the UK Government to pay in 'goods & services' from the British economy to the bearer of each pound note in circulation a 'pounds' worth of British goods or services on demand; or it is worthless.

If the millions of people all over the world who are currently holding sterling started to think that this promise would not, or could not, be kept and some 5% of them decided not to keep their sterling and to change their holdings into something else, there would be a 'run on the pound' and the pound would be in great difficulty and would drag down the UK economy in its wake.

The thing which holds the sterling system together is that obscure concept 'confidence'. Anything which would damage confidence, or which might damage confidence, in the pound must be avoided at all costs, the whole system is fragile.

Some people take the view that when you are in a situation which is precarious the best thing to do is to put a brave face on it and whistle in the dark and I suppose if you are in that situation that is probably good advice. The important thing however, is surely to avoid getting into that situation. We have all heard the saying "Safe as the Bank of England" adopting that position as an article of faith may be a form of whistling in the dark.

Sterling today, like the other big internationally exchanged currencies, is in a precarious situation and is completely out of the control of the UK Government, although the UK taxpayer is still entirely responsible for sterling's liabilities.

The UK Government has a National Dept in access of 1.5 trillion pounds. In other words they owe the rest of the world virtually every product and every service produced in the whole of Britain last year by everyone in Britain. So to pay off this debt every person in Britain would need to take no income for a full year and give everything they produced to the

Government. That is just the national debt, which is still being added to after 5 years of 'austerity'.

To meet the 'promise' on the front of the pound is a commitment in addition to the above, so how could the UK Government meet it today if there was a run on the pound? Where are our goods & services today to cover our promise? Britain was once a major manufacturing country, "the workshop of the world", but not today. The UK balance of trade has been in deficit for decades sustained by Scottish oil and services such as banking and Insurance.

Now if there were to be a run on the pound, UK banking and insurance would not be in great demand abroad, so would not help the UK in an attempt to stem the pressure on the pound and the UK just does not have the manufactured goods or natural recourses which would back up a failing pound. The idea of a 'lender of last resort' is also just mythology. It implies that some power, external to the domestic economy, is willing and has the resources to step in and meet such demand for payment. So where is this wealthy Good Samaritan? The bank of England we will be told. Really? Does the bank of England have such massive untapped reserves? Those of us who live in the real world know that this suggestion has no validity.

The reality is that the claim that an independent Scotland "could not share the UK pound", is in effect a claim that we "could not share the UK's debt" because in the real world that is what it means.

When seen in the clear light of reality, the absurdity of the claim is evident to all.

So let us be clear about this. Any country can use sterling as a currency and no British Government has any power over that. Using sterling means you are a creditor, not a borrower of sterling. Being responsible for sterling or 'sharing' in that responsibility means you are in debt to sterling users all over the world. So what exactly was it that the UK Government insisted we could not share? Not using the pound. They had no power over that. It was 'sharing' responsibility for the debt they were in reality objecting to.

That is the essence of the issue. Of course there is talk of being part of the BoE team which runs the BoE and sterling and sets interest rates and other minor tinkering with the system. We are told that if we were not participating in the pound we would not be able to play that role. Well, the first response to that is that we are currently in the sterling system and we can't see how much influence Scotland's Government has currently on the Board of the BoE. Secondly we note that the role played by the BoE Board is not a role of great significance, nor is it likely that a small country like Scotland would ever get a decisive role in the BoE board. What we do know is what the very high cost of 'sharing in sterling' is and would continue to be, for our community and for future generations of Scots.

The financial elite

Now let us return to the public statement made by David Cameron days after this currency ploy was started. He announced that irrespective of the outcome of the referendum, the UK Government was responsible for the National Debt. On the face of it, for many of us aware of the economic and financial situation, this statement just underlined what we knew to be the case and it made the direct link between sterling and the National Debt.

However, this statement undermined the strategy of "You can't share in our currency if you vote for independence" because in essence it meant "You can't have a share of our debt". Now if people had seen it in that light, then this project fear ploy would have fallen flat on its face. It most certainly would have failed to put fear into the Scottish electorate to tell them that they and their families would no longer have the privilege of paying off the banker's debt.

It was not the economic or financial reality which was used to spread fear and concern among the Scottish people; it was the 'distortion' of these issues which was designed to mislead the people.

Why then did David Cameron make the statement about the National Debt at that time?

True, he did not link the two issues and the media did not endlessly repeat his statement or link it to the currency issue either. Although it clearly is closely related to the currency issue and that is why it was raised at this time by the UK Prime Minister. However, it is unlikely that the Prime Minister did this entirely of his own volition. Again if we clear some of the fog away we can see that the Alistair Darling currency ploy, while very popular with the 'No Camp' and with Unionist politicians, would have been a source of some concern for the UK's real leaders who are in fact the financial capitalist elite who run modern Britain.

They are the small elite who run the banks, and the media and influence the UK establishment and the politicians. They are an important part of the iceberg which we don't see on the surface but which form the real power and substance of what we do see and they like to keep it that way. We do not know precisely what their views are because they do not stand for election or publish their manifesto; but we know from their media and from their puppet politicians what they see as their vital interests. So we know that they are keen on full interest being paid on all debts and they are determined that 'austerity' comes before people's living standards and their public health and welfare.

Now from what we know of the 'ruling' elite we know they are not interested in Scottish Independence, they are quite happy with Scotland being subjected to 'control' under the UK and EU systems which they have power over. So any UK Government policy designed to mislead the Scottish electorate and keep them in the UK would, on the face of it, be fine with them. However they saw the Darling currency ploy as dangerous. It was dangerous because it was in danger of bringing into focus some stark economic realities which they would have rather seen remain hidden.

The elite want Scotland to remain in the UK, but not at any price to them. What they want more than that, is the Scottish people tied for life into paying interest to meet sterling's debts. Now if they remain in the UK they get that as part of the deal, if however they leave the UK and stay responsible for sterling and its debts then the ruling elite will settle for that. What they certainly do not want is for the currency to be seen as unstable or vulnerable, because that could disrupt their system big time. They do not want the 'real' nature of the currency to be exposed to public view, because this is likely to cause people to question the whole corrupt system and of course they want no ambiguity about who is responsible for the National Debt.

Now the problem they saw with the Darling currency ploy was that it was implying that Scotland would not in future be part of the sterling system; and therefore would have no responsibility for the UK National Debt. That they could not ignore, because any ambiguity around this could easily spark of concern about the security of the pound and quickly lead to a run on the pound which could have dramatic consequences for their interests. Not that a run on the pound per se, would always damage their interest, indeed they have in the past organised runs on the pound when it suited them and made a lot of money out of it, as they do. However they need to control any such significant currency movements so they do not like movements, of that nature, which are not under their control.

Therefore David Cameron was told, to make a public statement about the National Debt, to make it clear so that there was no ambiguity whatever about who is responsible for meeting that debt, or the 'money markets' would react to the rhetoric coming out of the UK about Scotland not participating in sterling. Whatever the people may have thought about sterling; the elite had no doubt, Scotland's role in sterling was to share in the debt repayment and if the politicians in the UK did not want that, then they must publicly accept the full burden.

That view can help us to consider why David Cameron made the statement about the National Debt when he did. On the face of it, it does seem strange that he should make a point of publicly explaining that the UK Government were entirely responsible for the National Debt right at a time when he was engaged with the 'no campaign' in a ploy to cause fear and alarm in the 'Yes Camp'. His statement made clear that an independent Scotland, which was not formally in the sterling area, would be debt free. That was not the best way to spread fear and alarm to yes supporters.

The UK Prime Minister made that statement, at that time, in spite of its possible harmful effects on the currency ploy he was involved in, because he had no option. The powerful financial forces made it clear to him that he must clear up any doubts which the 'money markets' might have about this ambiguity surrounding the currency and the National Debt.

They, like Alex Salmond, knew that it was a bluff, but they thought it was a dangerous one which could undermine confidence in the pound. So they insisted that Cameron make it clear publicly that whatever the outcome of the referendum the UK Government would be responsible for the National Debt.

Exposing part of the iceberg

This political propaganda exercise in public gave us a glimpse of the under-water side of the iceberg. It exposed the fact that there are serious players in this game who are not registered to play in the normal way and that these players can have considerable influence on the game not least by the use of 'their' media.

Let us for a moment consider that among the most important of the hidden players are people who have vital interests in the current world financial system. Now we don't know much about these people and how they operate, but we can see some of their working methods in the shadow banking system, the so called money markets and the production of derivatives to extend their leverage in the fractional-reserve banking system. One thing we can be sure about is that they would not like to see major instability in international currencies which a run on the pound could cause, not that is, unless they were controlling it.

Now what do you think the 'ruling elite' would do if they believed that the Scottish Government were likely to go public with a statement that the UK Government did not want Scottish assistance with the UK National Debt?

You can be sure they would not want that. It presents them with three problems:

(a)   This debate exposes the National Debt issue to open examination.

(b)   This gives the Scots a good reason to 'escape' from contributing to a debt repayment.

(c)   This could trigger a run on the pound.

They could not stand aside and allow this petty squabble among politicians to burst open at the surface and possibly damage their vested interests. That would never do. They would make it clear to Cameron that such a public situation was unacceptable to them.

Scotland does not have a large GDP in world terms, however if the Scottish GDP was extracted for the UK GDP while at the same time the total debt level was static or rising, then the UK Debt – GDP ratio would rise significantly in one jump. Not a good idea, in a fragile system depending on confidence.

Such a significant change could easily trigger a fall in confidence in sterling and a run on the pound and once started such a move would be pretty unpredictable. I believe it is reasonable to assume that the financial ruling elite, who reacted last time by making David Cameron respond on the National Debt issue, may have some views to express to him about that.

Now, in any future referendum campaign, the Scottish Government should leave the UK Government in no doubt that they were not prepared to see sterling being used as a childish scare ploy as was done in the last referendum debate. If they then made it clear what their reaction to this would be and spelt it out to them, the UK Government, and therefore the financial elite would know the cost of a failure to agree.

The UK Government and the financial elite would understand that if an agreement could not be arrived at in a reasonable time, the Scottish Government would go public on the debt issue.

The UK Government must be under no illusion that they could repeat the currency scare scam they got away with last time with impunity. Once that was clear, then the light of reality might begin to shine into the UK Cabinet rooms, particularly if the financial elite were expressing concern.

This light might expose for them the ugly truth that an open public debate on this issue with the Scottish Government which was quite ready to explain the real substance of sterling and have it examined and analysed in public might not be in their best interests.

Scotland has no international legal obligation to contribute to the UK National Debt as indeed Mr Cameron himself publicly confirmed in 2014. So if the UK was refusing to make mutually satisfactory arrangements with Scotland, then we could reasonably take it that they did not want us to assist them with the UK National Debt.

In such circumstances the Scottish Government should express its disappointment, but move on publicly to its second option, which I will look at in detail in the chapter 3. The second option would mean Scotland using the pound for a period of time, but unofficially, and therefore with no responsibility for protecting or defending the pound. Rather like Panama uses the dollar today.

This situation would make it crystal clear that Scotland had no legal responsibility for any national debt. It would be like Norway a debt free nation in a Europe crippled with debt.

However let us return to option one and assume an agreement with the UK Government on a temporary agreement with sterling but not 'within' sterling. This would still leave Scotland with no legal responsibility for any of the UK national debt.

On the other hand, The Scottish people would be prepared to accept some 'moral' obligation to assist our friends and relations in the rest of the UK to meet their National Debt burden if we could do so, to our mutual satisfaction.

Now I can see this, as forming a reasonable negotiating position.

It may be that David Cameron and his political associates might not like that, it may be that they would not like to be seen making a u-turn on this issue publicly and as good negotiators, we should help them with their 'face-saving' but their financial masters will be more concerned about the danger of a public political dispute leading to a run on the pound than they will, about Scottish political independence or politicians face-saving.

The Scottish Government could reach a temporary deal on sterling with the UK Government, one which saved political face, while more importantly retained flexibility for each side to adopt an independent democratic decision of their respective parliaments after such a referendum.

The compromise deal would be built round two principles:

(a)   An independent Scotland would use sterling and operate for a 3 year period, not in the sterling zone (therefore not responsible for its debts) but in a special agreed relationship with sterling.

(b)   That Scotland would make a long term commitment to assist the r-UK with UK national Debt and that this commitment would be placed before an independent Scottish parliament for endorsement in the first session of an Independent Scottish parliament.

An agreement which disadvantages none

I take the view that such an agreement would be possible, that it could benefit the supporters of independence like myself, but equally would not be unfair to opponents of independence. I believe that such an approach would help supporters of a separate Scottish currency like myself, but would not be unfair to those who supported staying with sterling because after 3 years the Scottish parliament would be able to vote to stay with sterling if they believed it was in Scotland's interest to do so, or to adopt their own currency.

However the main advantage of this approach is that it would allow the independence issue to go ahead on its merits uncluttered with distortions and misrepresentations of economic and financial 'mythology'.

Democracy needs open, honest and free debate for it to operate. This attempt to mislead and distort important matters in order to spread fear and concern is the worse aspect of anti-democratic conduct.

The real issue is what should this temporary agreement contain and what could be done in Scotland to develop and examine this issue in depth so that the Scottish people and Scottish parliament would be in a position to make a genuine democratic decision on this issue at the end of the 3 year agreement.

In Chapter three we will look at the situation we would have if the UK Government refused to enter into an agreement with the Scottish Government on the currency issue. Before we do this we will look further into the nature of any temporary agreement which Scotland should make with the UK Government on this matter.

If our first option to make such a temporary agreement is to be advanced there is a lot of work needs to be done into every aspect of it, because the main reason for having a temporary agreement is to give time and opportunity to develop a better more stable system for the long term.

Chapter 2

Sharing UK Debt

In the last chapter I claimed that Scotland had no legal obligation to pay off any of the UK's debt, indeed the UK Prime Minister had publicly announced that the UK Government was responsible for the whole of this debt whether or not Scotland was independent.

So that being the case, why should a future Scottish Parliament agree to pay anything toward assisting the r-UK with meeting this debt?

Some of the old 'Better Together' gang made a baseless claim that if Scotland did not pay 'its' share of the UK national debt then it would be isolated internationally by all other nations, treated as a pariah and with total disrespect, as untrustworthy, unreliable and not entitled to normal diplomatic courtesies. A country placed in that position internationally which can't be trusted to pay its debts, would get a reputation which would cost it dearly.

That exaggerated claim, like much of the 'project fear' assertions from Better Together, has no validity. If no country or organisation has a valid legal claim against the Scottish Government for one single penny, then simple logic tells you that it is not possible for Scotland to 'fail to pay' any of its debts. That would only be possible if it had debts.

I did take the view never the less, in the last chapter, that Scotland should offer the r-UK a long-term deal to help them with their UK National Debt burden. I believe that there are several very sound reasons why we should do that, but a legal obligation is not one of them.

I will set-out here some reasons for offering the r-UK a long-term assistance deal to help them with their National Debt.

Moral Obligation

I use the term 'moral' not in the sense of a duty which requires to be met, but more in the sense of a social commitment. The Scots, in general are known to take a more collective view of society than some other people do.

Margaret Thatcher, for example, said there was no such thing as society, merely a collection of individuals. However that view would not be widely accepted in Scotland. Burn's view that we are "aw Jock Tamson's bairns" is more likely to find acceptance here.

Scottish Independence from the Westminster Establishment, contrary to much of what we have heard from the opposition and their media, even from some foolish Scots, who should know better; is not about being anti-English or anti-British. The Scottish people's demand for independence is motivated by democratic and social needs, it is a positive objective not a negative one. The idea that Scots, in their hundreds of thousands should be motivated by such a negative attitude is in fact insulting to the Scottish people and is naive and foolish.

Those of us who want to take control of Scotland's economy and resources in order to ensure they are better distributed among all the people living in Scotland are not motivated by anti-English or anti-British sentiment. On the contrary many of us would rejoice to see the rest of the UK make big changes in their economic ideas similar to the way we want to make such changes in Scotland. Indeed many Scots were delighted with the considerable support, against strong media pressure, which Jeremy Corbyn achieved in the Labour leadership election, when he presented an anti-austerity position.

The idea of the people in the rest of the UK recognising that neo-liberal ideology has to be rejected and 'austerity' with it, is pleasing for many of us Scots. We have no desire to see any family anywhere in the UK suffer from unemployment and poverty. To suggest or imply otherwise is vile, and entirely without foundation.

The Scottish people have many friends and relatives living elsewhere in the UK. The Better Together gang acknowledged this, but went on to distort this fact by claiming that Scottish independence would damage such relationships. On the contrary our close relationship with the people in England, Wales and Ireland will be strengthened by Scotland having its own more compassionate Government and by us making real meaningful commitments to our neighbours rather than empty expressions of affection.

We all saw how worthless the empty expressions of affection were towards Scotland from English Tories in the Referendum campaign. When on the very day of the result, Cameron announced his plan for EVEL which would strip Scottish MPs of some of their rights in the UK Parliament. This exposed the hypocrisy of these very same people who previously had expressed affection for us Scots when they wanted us to vote against independence.

As well as the r-UK being our close neighbours, and our friends and relatives, we have a shared common history which for a lot of us, in the older generation particularly, is very real; the fight against Hitler at home and abroad, the establishment of the NHS, the development of the post-war economy when real redistribution of income across the UK did take place. That shared history is real, although it is now somewhat faded since Westminster Governments of both colours have long abandoned social responsibility and are redistributing from the people to the super rich.

I believe that like me, most Scots will feel a moral obligation to help our r-UK neighbours with their crippling National Debt burden. This is a natural inclination, irrespective of any legal requirement. If we saw a neighbour drowning in the swimming pool would we not try to help?

There is no question about it, I am confident that the Scottish people will want to help here and will feel a moral obligation to do so. How we can best do this however, needs consideration. If our neighbour is going under due to heavy commitments to a 'loan-shark' who is demanding that he hands over his earnings to comply with their steep interest demands; we should help our neighbour, but we should find a better way to do it than to take out a loan from the same loan-shark.

So the first and most important reason, why we should help the r-UK with their National Debt problem is a moral obligation to them which few Scots would disagree with.

Economic sense

There are very sound economic reasons why it makes sense for Scotland to help the r-UK with its crippling debt problem, but in order to explain these it will be helpful if I give a wee bit of attention to economic theory so that you can understand where I am coming from and hopefully come with me.

In the book 'Moving On' a distinction is made between economic 'theory' and economic 'mythology'*. The distinction being that a theory was a rational explanation which could be tested and measured. While mythology was assertions which one had to accept as an article of faith, such assertions were not open to rational examination or measurement. We argued that Keynesian economic theory was an example of the former, while neo-liberal assertions were an example of the latter.

In that book we gave some examples of Keynesian theory in practice in the post-war Attlee Government.

This explains how it is possible for a country, which has unemployment, or underemployment and available natural resources, to use public investment to create wealth. This theory has been subjected to testing, has been tested in Britain and elsewhere, and has been shown to work effectively.

One of the main reasons why Scotland needs independence, and indeed control over its currency, is to implement the public investment now required in Scotland, to grow its economy. The Keynesian approach is to 'grow your way' out of economic depression such as the UK and Scotland have been experiencing. It is obvious that if Scotland can bring significant growth into the Scottish economy it will create a lot more wealth. Now, I and many others know that this can be done and how it can be done, so we are keen to get on with it in a rational way and not be held back by neo-liberal austerity.

On the other hand the UK Government is strongly under the influence of neo-liberal mythology and is determined to drive home the austerity project; which is in effect the direct opposite from the way the economy has to go. In such circumstances there can be no meeting of minds, no compromise solution. Our offer of help must be an offer to the people of the UK and may not be what their elected Government might want us to offer. However in offering help it is for the party making the donation to decide how it will offer assistance, the recipient has the option of accepting or rejecting the donation.

Now any help we give to the r-UK must be 'real' if it is to be of any value to the people. The UK national Debt is identified in money terms, as is the enormous annual interest, which is paid to 'service' this debt.

The diagram below shows this debt and who it is owed to:

The actual amount of the UK National debt is increasing every day and in July 2015 was standing at £1,510,569,532,546. Everyone knows that this debt can't be repaid so the real burden is the heavy interest payments, which again in July 2015 stood at £1,865* per household per year for the whole of the UK.

So if the Scots were not allowed to be responsible for Sterling, and therefore not required to support the UK economy which is behind it; then each Scottish household would have saved £1,865 in July for last year, and an amount exceeding that next July and every future July in interest payments. If interest rates should rise, as is expected, this would of course push this figure up substantially. Needless to say the politicians who insisted that an independent Scotland could not share their pound, did not make this clear to the Scottish people, nor did they advise the rest of the people in the UK that they had just promised to put that significant extra interest burden onto them.

This is why a long-term deal on Scottish assistance with the UK debt burden should be of great interest to any prudent UK politician or economist.

Now it would be of no value to the British people if we Scots were to take out our own Scottish National Debt with the same 'Loan sharks' in order to pay nearly £2,000 per household per annum towards interest in the UK National Debt, and we would be very foolish to do so. If we stayed within the sterling system and remained responsible for its commitments, we would be doing just that and in addition taking on the responsibility for sterling's own commitments, which we would have no control over.

It would however be entirely possible for us to offer a long-term trade agreement with the r-UK in which we supply real goods and services to the r-UK market at discounted prices to help them with their debt interest payments. Such a deal would offer the British people 'real wealth' of the equivalent or greater value than the £2,000 per household, rather than us paying money to international bankers on their behalf.

If we were to do this it would be of substantial 'real' value to the r-UK economy and could be done by us, to our economic advantage also. In other words we could give our neighbours a real help which could be done without us getting into debt and which could even help our economy too. Now that is what I call a real 'win – win' deal.

Scottish power

Let us take renewable power, to give a practical example of how this would work for both communities.

We know that England in particular is concerned about its future power supplies. We have just seen the very public deal they have done with Xi Jinping, President of the Chinese People's Republic. This commitment they have made to a French company and two Chinese companies to provide power to around 12 million people by constructing two nuclear power stations at a cost of some £25 billion each is an extremely expensive commitment. Therefore we must conclude that the UK Government is very worried about their future power supplies. What is less then clear, is the full costs of this power to the consumers. It has been estimated that this nuclear deal will produce electricity at three times the world average cost of electricity from nuclear power. The agreement itself acknowledges that power prices will be high and sets them at £92.5 per megawatt hour as opposed to the present cost of £40 per megawatt hour. That is more than double the current high price.* This is a long- term commitment which leaves the UK with expensive and dangerous power provision and dependent on a foreign Super-Power.

Now if we take into account that the population of England is over 53 million then this huge price for supplying electricity alone to well below a quarter of the people, and driving up prices in this dramatic way, clearly demonstrates that England has need of cheaper power supplies. Power supplies are at the very core of industrial production costs. TATA steel has made it clear that one of the big costs (another one being the high pound which we will address later) which has forced it to close down steel production in the UK is current power costs, which it claims are the highest in Europe.

Now Scotland just happens to have some of the most favourable renewable power sources in Europe. We have a small population so our own domestic requirement for power is small in international terms, so we have a great potential for producing and exporting power cheaply.

If, for example, we were to supply renewable power to the r-UK at discounted prices across an improved grid system to Northern Ireland and England; we could use this improved grid system to supply European markets via France and the South of Ireland.

If we did this, we could take economic advantage of our considerable natural resources in renewable energy and by using our high level of technical knowledge we could invest at a high level to cater for a larger market. If we did this 'economies of scale' and high productivity would enable us to product power at a low marginal unit cost and therefore to provide the r-UK with energy at a generous discounted rate lower than international market prices; while at the same time making a reasonable return for our investment by our supply to the wider European market.

The economics are clear. Scotland can, and will, take advantage of this natural wealth on our doorstep. If we do it just to provide for our own population the initial investment costs will be lower but the unit costs of production will be higher initially. However if we do it on a much bigger scale the investment costs will rise but the unit production cost will fall and we will be able to produce large amounts of clean, safe and cheap power for ever.

Now the question is, can the UK Government, which is prepared to ask the people in England to pay the Chinese, more than twice what they are currently paying for electricity, refuse to co-operate with a Scottish Government which is prepared to offer them a reduction on the current price of power? Scotland could provide large scale, clean, reliable and safe power to our neighbours if we sat down and negotiated satisfactory terms.

This is only one example of a number of real possibilities for such trading deals, there are possibilities in oil and gas and in a wide range of industry and manufacturing where Scotland has the potential for efficient development of an industry beyond its domestic market and a long term deal with a bigger close neighbour would work to mutual satisfaction and in which Scotland could offer discounts in a 'special relationship' which would avoid EU challenge and could help the r-UK with its high interest repayments on its National Debt.

I believe that this sort of approach leading to a long-term trade deal could enable Scotland to develop our economy while also helping our r-UK neighbours with their National Debt problem. At the moment the high interest on UK National Debt, is being met from the products in the 'real' economy and in so doing, is reducing the amount of real resources available to the people in real earnings and the social wage (i.e. health care, education etc). Therefore if we want to be of assistance to the people of the r-UK, as opposed to the bankers to whom we have no moral obligation, then we must find ways to give real help to the people and try to avoid this help being siphoned off by the bankers.

The Wider Market

Scotland is a small country, population wise, so it does not need to have a large impact on world markets in order to do well. Norway is of a similar size and does not have a large impact on world markets in any aspect, but it is the wealthiest (per capita) country in the world by some definitions.

Scotland does not need to have a dominant position in any world market, but it does need to have a range of natural resources, products and services, extensive enough to be flexible in world markets and to adjust to changes in demand. Fortunately Scotland has exactly that.

Scotland today, like the rest of the UK, and most of Europe has considerable unemployment and underemployment. I am not talking here about recorded 'registered' unemployed, which is bad enough, but more importantly about under-employment such as 'zero-hours contract' and low-wage meaningless low productivity abuse of labour. If Scotland started to invest in real value employment providing high wage, high productivity production, then the Scottish people would gain a great deal from this, and could, for a number of years expand its economy and wealth on that basis. People must not lose sight of the obvious point, particularly for small local businesses, one man's wage; is another man's 'demand'. So if you need more demand for your business, higher wages in the area is the best way to get it.

Now just to deal with another economic distortion, the above outline of the Scottish economy is true, with or without oil and gas production. The suggestion that Scotland's economy and future is dependent on oil is another big distortion, this is just not true, Scotland does not depend on oil; although oil and gas production are an important part of Scotland's rich natural resources and will be so for at least the next 50 years. The oil industry is not one which Scotland's long-term economic future depends on, because oil does not have a long-term future. However much the oil price may change in the future Scotland's economy will depend on its diversity not on any single resource, valuable as any such resource may be.

In growing and developing its world market Scotland needs to have access to and involvement in the UK market. Indeed access to the UK market can in many situations be related to Scotland's wider access to other markets. For example, Scotland currently has a valuable international market in whisky and the fact that whisky has a strong base in British culture helped it to develop its wider European and International appeal.

The Land Border with England and the close cultural links with the other three countries in the British Isles determine a need for good relationships and is something which most Scots would be keen to maintain. This means, of course, that Scotland would have a continuing interest in an efficient transport system through England in terms of high quality rail service from the Scottish border to the Channel Tunnel as well as good airport facilities in England for the movement of goods and people.

There are therefore very good reasons for Scotland to have good trading relationships with r-UK and to strengthen such links where possible. A long-term special trading deal, supported by the Scottish Parliament and up-dated from time to time by the two Governments would not only be a means of giving assistance to the r-UK with their debt burden but may be a good long-term way of helping trade relationships. It is likely that because of the special link between Scotland and the r-UK such a 'special' trade agreement would be permitted with-in the EU rules as a pass-on from the unitary state.

History should teach the leadership in the UK Government that when a people decide that the union with Britain is over, then the wisest thing for the British leadership to do is to accept that situation and move towards preserving what links and ties can be maintained in the best interests of both countries. Childish petulance and refusing to co-operate is not a very mature attitude for National leaders.

Scotland r-UK agreement

On the basis of exploring a long-term agreement of this nature it would make a lot of sense for any UK Government to take very seriously a discussion with the Scottish Government, prior to any future referendum, about coming to such an agreement. I have no doubt that many more mature thinkers in England are aware that the writing is on the wall as regards the future of the United Kingdom. They can undoubtedly see that a sensible and rational division, arrived at democratically is the way forward.

If the sane voices in England manage to get a hearing then there should be a good basis for an agreement on these issues between the Scottish and UK Government, because there are no fundamental issues which should prevent it. The opposition is primarily ideological and irrational. That of course does not mean that is will be easy to overcome, but it does mean that it is vulnerable to clear rational ideas, which we must be prepared to advance at every opportunity.

From the Scottish Government's perspective it would be helpful if a firm agreement could be drawn up based on Scotland using sterling within a special temporary agreement, primary for external exchange for a specified period, following a positive vote for independence after a referendum.

The outline of such an understanding would be that Scotland would not be an integral part of sterling, but would operate a special temporary agreement with the r-UK Government in relation to Scotland's use of Sterling. An understanding would need to be arrived at which would divide the assets of sterling and the banking system in some agreed way, and reach agreement with the Scottish Government about a nationalized Scottish National Bank (SNB) for Scotland working with the BoE concerning the establishment of a full-reserve Scottish pound on par with the pound sterling operating as the sole legal currency in Scotland. While Scotland used sterling for international trade.

The reserves of the Scottish pound would be held in the SNB which would also be responsible for money supply and Scottish monetary policy.

Scottish Government public expenditure would be in the Scot's pound which would be controlled by the balance of public assets held in relation to the public money supply. The SNB should work with the BoE as regards information sharing on reserves held by the SNB and this should mean that Scottish Government investment, covered by public assets should be a matter for the Scottish Government alone, but should not be a matter for concern for the BoE because they would be able to see that the Scottish currency was maintained on a full-reserve basis.

On the other side of the coin, Scotland, which has no responsibility for UK National Debt would offer a long-term special trading agreement between Scotland and r-UK to last 5 years and be renegotiated on a 5 year basis. This agreement would be used to harmonise the two economies to some extent, to widen trade relationships, and to allow Scotland to assist the r-UK with its high ND.

If such a deal could be arrived at as proposed above, the Scottish Government would agree to recommend the deal to the Scottish Parliament immediately following their resumption of full power. This would then provide the possibility for a pre-referendum agreement on currency to be established between the two Governments and published by them.

Such a development would take the currency issue right out of the independence debate, and would allow the independence issue to be considered on its merits and not by scare tactics about money and savings and pensions etc; I believe this would be a great advance on what happened in 2014.

I consider that this approach provides the possibility of reaching an understanding on currency by both Governments, which would leave open the opportunity for the Scottish people to discuss the currency and banking system they wanted for their future and for the future of their children and grand-children in the New Scotland.

Such an arrangement would not close the door on any side of the debate on currency because in effect the final sovereign decision on currency would be made by the Scottish people in an Independent Scottish Parliament after Scotland achieved its political independence. There would then be the opportunity for those who want Scotland to go back into the sterling system, to advance their case for that, before the temporary agreement finished.

Scottish Public Investment

Since staying out of sterling and operation a full-reserve currency in Scotland would keep the Scottish people debt free, and would allow the Scottish Government to invest, interest free, in Scottish public assets I doubt very much that many Scots would want to return to sterling and all its problems, but that option would be there.

Just to make this issue clear let us take a wee look at some of to-days problems in the Scottish economy. I have said that Scotland needs a range of economic activity if it is going to survive in the world market today. If that is to happen it is urgent that the Scottish Government has real economic power to get involved in the market if and when a situation arises which requires quick attention. This is important if we are going to be able to save what is left of our manufacturing base.

We have all seen what happened in shipbuilding and the most recent example of the miracle of Ferguson Marine in Port Glasgow. Here was a doomed ship yard which went bankrupt and made its 70 employees redundant, amongst which were some young apprentices. Well this was not a new story for Scotland, nor was it new for shipbuilding in the UK. Indeed this was the last none-military ship builder in the UK.

The Scottish Government found a like-minded private investor in Jim McColl who bought the dilapidated plant from the liquidator and drew up a rescue plan. By recognising the potential, Jim McColl set to work on a development plan and invested money in the project. Not only did he find work for the 70 staff, including the apprentices who were under notice but he now has expanded the workforce currently with 150 employees with plans to employ 1,300 in the medium term including 150 apprentices. His long-term plans envisage a major new development of the yard to handle considerably technologically advanced none-military vessels with many more employees.

Now this is great news for the local people, for the Scottish Government and for the Scottish economy. This was no miracle however, it was simple economics and the Keynesian multiplier effect of it has not been fully developed yet whereby the increase in local employment and local income being spent in the area will stimulate growth in the economy and multiply that growth by increasing demand.

We can see exactly the same thing in the steel industry in the UK and Scotland today. Scotland has already lost most of its steel industry and it looks like losing all of it. However that need not be.

If we could find £billions overnight, to 'save' RBS then for a very very much smaller sum of public money we could secure jobs in the steel industry which are very much in jeopardy in Scotland today and reinvest to secure a future for Scottish steel. There are of course problems and real investment is required, but with commitment and the resources to invest there is no doubt that the Scottish Government could rescue a Scottish steel industry and help it to develop. Provided it had the power that an independent Scotland with control of its own currency would have.

Indeed I have seen a letter in the Sunday Herald* by John Smart from Lossiemouth a metallurgist by profession who suggests the Dalzell plant should be fed by melting scrap metal from ship breaking, oil rig decommissioning etc. He indicates that such a process would be practical because there should be enough of the right sort of scrap which would require less heating time and could be produced at a competitive price for industrial use.

Now I do not know about the practicalities of this; but the economics are beautiful and so is the progressive thinking behind it, so appropriate for a small inventive nation like ours. This would preserve steel making, while helping other small businesses, while improving the environment, while helping a current workforce with a problem, while helping the economy. This sort of thing could be addressed by a Scottish Government with economic power, because it is perhaps too small scale for a UK Government, but ideal for a Scottish one.

This indeed is one of the great advantages of a smaller country in world market terms. If that country has a well educated work force, if it has natural resources available, if it has industrial and business experience and a helpful Government it can be flexible enough to identify a niche in the international market and move into it quickly in a way that a larger economy can't. That is perhaps why small countries are highly successful in the international market today. They seem to be flexible enough to respond quickly to market opportunities. It is also undoubtedly the reason why some of these small countries have the highest income per capita in the world today, not the large super-powers.

UK Government decision

If the UK Government rejects an approach such as I suggest here, after Scottish Government contacts have discussed it with them, then we will know that they are not interested in a reasonable outcome of the issue. We can be sure that they will only do so because they want, once again, to use a 'project fear' attack on the Scottish people by exploiting uncertainty and by using misleading and distorted implications about currency. The warning to the Scottish Government and the Scottish people should be obvious. We all have to learn from our mistakes, but having learned we must make sure we do not repeat them. Faced with UK Government obstinacy on this the Scottish Government must recognise what it means and must not allow the UK Establishment and their media to play that card on the Scottish people again.

The Scottish Government must make sure that the UK Government clearly understand that a failure to reach agreement on the currency issue with the Scottish Government before the independence campaign starts, will lead directly to the Scottish Government adopting another approach entirely which we will look at in the next chapter.

If the UK Government were to recognise that such an approach by them again, would be firmly met by the currency issue and the debt being exposed in an open way in the public arena, they would realise the danger. Any polls showing that the Scottish people were likely to vote 'yes' would lead to international speculation about the reliability of the UK National Debt. This would place responsibility for a likely run on the pound in the UK Government's hands.

Even if the UK Government were prepared to take that risk, their masters in the ruling elite may not be so rash and may instruct the UK Government to do a deal.

So I belief that such a political understanding can be achieved because both sides have objectives which they can obtain, or avoid, by such an agreement. However since this outcome depends on actions of others outwith Scotland's control we need to have a second option available to employ if this reasonable approach is not accepted. Indeed the absence of a ready alternative option for the Scottish Government means that they would show a weak negotiating position and may invite the UK Government to reject their offers.

There can be no question of Scotland again playing the role of some suppliant begging the UK Government to accept what we claim is in their interest as well as ours. That is how things appeared to be last time.

This time this issue must be entirely within our control and in no way depending on the views of the UK Government. Our first option should be to offer an agreement of the type described above which must be an honest effort to reach agreement; but if this is rejected we must move on without hesitation to our second option, so that the Scottish people and the people elsewhere in the UK, know exactly what our post referendum position on this important issue will be.

I now move to chapter 3, where I explain what I believe should be our second option, should the UK leadership fail to accept our offer of option one.

* Andy Anderson & Ronnie Morrison 'Moving On' page 21

* Published UK Government Statistics

* Jonathon Porritt 'Energy 15-10-15

* Sunday Herald 25-10-15 Letters

Chapter 3

Option two

If the UK Government should refuse to co-operate with the Scottish Government on reaching an agreement on currency before a future referendum, we must recognise such refusal for what it is; a clear declaration that they intend once again to use the 'currency issue' in a renewed 'project fear' campaign.

The project fear policy depends on ignorance and misunderstanding of the currency issue. We must therefore address this issue head on, identify it for what it really is, and explain our position in relation to it.

We would be foolish indeed to ignore this, or to allow the project fear manipulators to get away with this trick once again

So the Scottish Government needs to be in a position to identify exactly the policy it intends to follow.

As soon as our approach to the UK Government for an agreement on this issue is rejected we need to announce that an independent Scotland will do the following:

(1)   Scotland will establish a Scottish National Bank (SNB) and will reform the banking system.

(2)   Scotland will use a new full-reserve Scottish Pound in the Scottish domestic economy.

(3)   Scotland will use sterling as its main foreign exchange currency for the first 3 years after independence

(4)   The Scottish Government will keep open the offer to reach an agreement with the UK Government over financial issues including possible Scottish assistance to the UK over its National Debt

By making it clear that we are going ahead with our own currency arrangements and do not intend to wait for the UK Government to come to an understanding with us we will show the Scottish people that we mean business and have a clear way forward on this issue.

This will also place the UK National Debt item squarely where it lies; that it is a UK problem and not a Scottish one. If there is to be no rational agreement between the Scottish and UK Government then the UK will have to find a solution to the ND problem without Scotland's help.

What is wrong with sterling?

If we are setting out a financial and economic plan for the country we need to be able to do two things in order to win people's support. First to explain clearly what is wrong with the current situation; and then to explain how our changes will make improvements.

Most people recognise that there is something fundamentally wrong with the existing banking system. They can see the problems in Europe and the US, all stemming from the same banking collapse in 2008. They have observed the 'austerity' programmes being addressed in many countries, causing great distress, year after year, yet having no success anywhere.

People know that the banks caused the problem and that Governments everywhere gave them billions in taxpayer's money to resolve the problem, but to no avail. They may not understand that the four big banks in the UK are 'Zombie' Banks, by Onaran's definition*, in that they have liabilities greater than their assets and should not legally be allowed to trade; but they know that the banks are involved in crooked transactions like the LIBOR scandal, and that they are paying themselves huge bonuses with taxpayers money.

When we say this is a problem caused by the unregulated so called 'free market' fractional-reserve private banking system, people know that is true; but perhaps they need to know how the system has operated and how this came about.

The root cause of this banking collapse is the 'fractional-reserve' system itself. The fractional reserve system is inherently unstable. The system to be blunt is based on a fraud. It is an old fraud, first discovered by bankers centuries ago, but it is still a fraud. It works in the following simple way. Bankers discovered that people who put their money into banks have a tendency not to keep drawing it all out. Indeed they seldom want to draw out all their money. If you take a large number of people and measure over time the extent to which they draw money out of the bank you might discover that this only amounted to some 10% of the money in the bank on average.

Bankers of course discovered this a long time ago, and realised that it could be very useful to them.

Now let us, at this point, make a comparison between a bank and a mutual building society. I do this to contrast a fractional-reserve system; with a full-reserve system.

Suppose you have a mutual building society which does business by getting funds from people's savings and lending these funds to people who want to buy a house.

A mutual building society of the type we had a lot of in the UK a few years back operated on a 'full-reserve basis: Which meant that they could only lend to borrowers from the deposits that savers had put in, while maintaining a small reserve for business activity.

This of course limited the amount that a building society could lend to customers to the amount of savings it had taken in. This did not seriously inhibit mortgages in the UK; indeed most private housing in the UK was financed this way.

Now let's look at a bank which is not restricted in that way. It has discovered that it need retain only a 'fraction' let's say 10% of the money savers have put into the bank and it can lend out more, more indeed than it has. Is this clear? It means that with a mutual building society it can lend out £90 of every £100 of savers money, keeping 10% for withdrawals; but a fractional-reserve bank can use the £100 deposited as representing the 10% fractional reserve, and lend out £900 at interest on the strength of the actual deposit. This means that a bank can lend out money, which it does not have,'phantom money' indeed, and charge interest on it.

That is at the very core of the fractional-reserve system. Banks can create 'money' now-a-days by computer, which does not exist in any meaningful sense and they can charge interest on this phantom money. Now of course, when you have banks working together, you can see how this fractional reserve system can be extended. Then bank 'products' such as derivatives are created and eventually used by banks as part of their fractional-reserve. Now a 'derivative' is in effect a 'promise' which derives from the bank's fractional reserves. So it is in effect a promise of a promise. One can see how the system is wide open to abuse and without tight regulation it is extensively abused. So history has shown that banks, which operate such a system need to be strictly controlled and regulated by Government.

However Margaret Thatcher introduced 'reforms' to the financial system in the City of London which she called the Big Bang reforms in 1986 which were designed to sweep away banking regulation and allow 'free enterprise' to have free reign in the UK banking system.

This of course meant that banks were no longer there to provide a service to the economy under Government supervision and control, but were private businesses out to get what they could and make the highest profit they could for their private shareholders and the public, and the national economy was of no concern to them. If you put these two things together (a) the ability to create phantom money and (b) the right to make as much profit as you can irrespective of the consequences; and if at the same time, drastically reduce Government controls and regulation, it is not surprising that you get problems.

Thatcher's neo-liberal view on this was not confined to the UK, indeed Ronald Reagan, joined Thatcher in the ceremony of cutting the ribbon of the Big Bang and freeing capitalism from State restriction in London and later started to instigate the same anti-regulation for banks in the USA. In December that year the first assault was made in the USA on the interpretation of the Glass-Steagall Act, which eventually led to its repeal some years later.*

The Glass-Steagall Act was brought in by President Franklin D Roosevelt in 1933 after the Wall Street crash following a banking collapse in 1929. The purpose of the Act was to ensure that such banking irresponsibility had to be curbed by regulation to try to control too much abuse of the system and to protect the public interest.

It is widely recognised by economists everywhere that this new neo-liberal system is fatally flawed. Many of them know that it is the fractional-reserve system itself which is the problem. However they realise that it can't be changed without major upheaval and redistribution and those in power will not allow this.

If however Scotland is building a new banking system with a new currency this would give us the opportunity to entirely avoid this dangerous flaw and build it clean. Such a currency could be sustainable, but only if retained under Government control and proper regulation. So we will need to create a full-reserve currency for the new Scotland, and we will need to ensure that it is protected from the wolves in the capitalist international banking system.

The sterling system is at the epicentre of the international fractional-reserve banking system so we need to make people understand that we will never escape from banking problems if we stay within that flawed system. The banking crisis of 2008 will return again, because its basic cause has not been addressed. It is like living on an active volcano it is just a matter of time.

In addressing the difference between fractional-reserve, and full-reserve, banking, Ronnie Morrison produced an illustration in our book 'Moving On' which I am reproducing here:

The two main banking systems - Fractional Reserve and Full Reserve - Stability Comparison

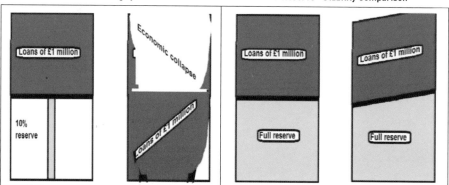

This illustration concentrates on the weakness of the reserves which 'support' the fractional-reserve banking system and illustrate how weak they are, particularly if they are part of a chain of internationally related banks where if one collapses it can cause a domino effect and bring a number of others tumbling after it. I reproduce this here because I think it is useful to illustrate the vulnerability of the fractional-reserve banking system.

However, I want to introduce another set of illustrations on the same subject, but looked at from a different angle examining the inputs and outputs from the banking system. In the following illustrations you can look at the banking system as a water tank with money, like water flowing in and out. This gives another view into the weakness and vulnerability of the fractional-reserve system.

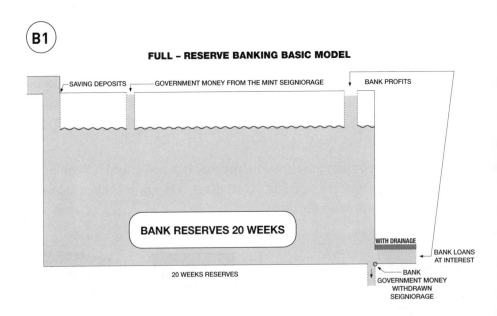

FULL – RESERVE BANKING BASIC MODEL

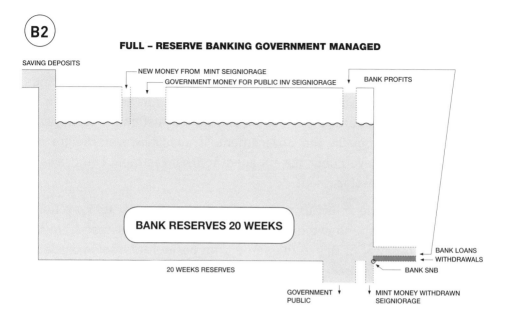

In both the full-reserve system and the fractional reserve system the outputs are controlled by the bank at the right hand bottom corner of the tank.

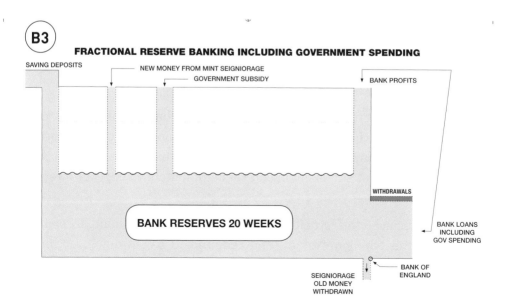

The bank, in our Scottish National Bank example, in the full-reserve system, has complete control of all money outputs for the Government and the private sector. On private input from savers the bank pays interest on deposits, which it adjusts to encourage more or less savings as required. The bank does not pay interest on any money put in by Government 'seigniorage' nor does it charge interest on the withdrawal of such seigniorage by the Government. It does however require the Government to have public assets equal to its investment withdrawals, other than cash replacement.

This is made clear by using two illustrations: One (b1) excludes Government input and withdrawals (other than supply of cash from the mint, and renewal of this in the same time period) this 'seigniorage' is neutral in that it puts in and takes out new money for old, not changing the total. This amounts to around 3% of total money supply. Two (b2) is the same illustration with Government money injected and withdrawn at the same amount for Government investment. This money is also seigniorage, although used for a different 'economic' purpose. It is also neutral and is not subject to interest.

If you study these illustrations you will see that in the present fractional-reserve system, (b3), the bank, the Bank of England, has a larger total output than its total input. This is to illustrate that the BoE, and other banks can create 'phantom' money by issuing loans on 'fractions' of the real deposits it holds, it does not even have control over the total amount of loans issued by banks in the UK.

The BoE is not therefore, in a position to ensure that total input and total output are kept in line. The Government is supplying financial support to the system, and paying interest on its own investments, which is another kind of subsidy, but still is not in control of total money supply or interest reinvested.

This is precisely the problem. The Government, although forced to subsidies the banking system, and required to bail it out if, or more accurately when, it collapses; has no control of the banking system or the money supply. These important economic controls are in the hands of private, internationally owned banks, although the responsibility for the currency,still remains with the UK Government.

Does Sterling cause economic problems?

The next unsustainable weakness of the present system is that the flaws in the financial system are being allowed to cripple the real economy through the austerity programme. Most people know that this is so and want to put a stop to it, but are not entirely clear how to go about this.

We need to address this and explain what the new Scotland's economic policy should be and how it can reject austerity and rebuild the economy and how this can be measured. So that people can see, not only how we intend to see a big improvement in Scotland's economic achievements after independence, but also how our claims on this can be measured by them.

This raises a fundamental question. What is economic success in a country? How can you measure it?

When Adam Smith wrote 'The Wealth of Nations"*, which is generally accepted as the first book on economic theory, he was not concerned with individual wealth, his focus was on the collective wealth of the nation. This seems the wise approach. So if we want to know about the wealth of Britain we need to try to measure the living standards of the people as a whole not just one section.

Viewed in this way there is no doubt that the British economy is failing, and has increased its extent of failure since the banking crash in 2008. Because real living standards for the great majority of the population have fallen, while the income of the very richest has increased at a phenomenal rate. So in real economic terms Britain is becoming poorer not wealthier, its economy is failing. GDP figures, by themselves, are not a good measure of this. The best measure is the real standard of living of the majority of the people, and a good way to measure that is to look at the conditions of the poorest 50%.

This is not of course limited to Britain. Economists are looking at this on a wider international scale. Some of the world's best recognised economists such as Joseph Stiglitz, ex-chief Economist at the World Bank and Nobel prize winner in economics, and indeed advisor to the Scottish Government, in his book 'Freefall' refers to the "sinking of the global economy"* following the banking crisis, and the steps taken to 'correct' the situation.

The most recent Nobel Prize for economics was awarded to Professor Angus Deaton* of Princeton in the USA, but who comes from Edinburgh. In his work on "consumption, poverty and welfare" the professor has looked at the links between individual consumption and demand implications for the whole economy. In his book "The Great Escape" he looks at 'Health, Wealth and the Origins of Inequality'. Not surprisingly Professor Deaton finds that inequality is increasing and real incomes for very many are falling undermining demand and growth in Western economies.

There is a great deal of knowledge and data which now supports the view that a fairer distribution of income is necessary, in order to develop the economy and that inequality is holding the process back. In real economic terms it is not austerity that Scotland needs, but the very opposite. Not a re-distribution for poor to the wealthy as austerity is in reality; but a re-distribution from the super-rich to the community.

In our previous book 'Moving On' we dealt in some detail with the Keynesian economic policies* employed by the post war Attlee Government, which had the advantage of having John Maynard Keynes as an economic advisor. We show how the Keynesian economic policies that Government followed, made them the most economically successful British Government ever and left us with a great heritage such as the NHS which is now being undermined.

What was vital for Keynes and the policies he knew were required to lift the war shattered UK economy out of the mess it was in, was to take full control of the financial system, and to that end, one of the first steps of the Attlee Government was to nationalize the Bank of England in order to take control of money supply and monitory policy which they required to have, if they were to put in the public investment that they needed from the UK's debt ridden, war torn economy.

History shows that they did a remarkable job of this and turned round the UK economy in a very short time period. This is a lesson in economics which the Labour Party should be proud of but many of them appear to be ignorant of it. All economists need to study carefully what the Attlee Government's economic policy achieved and learn from it. Yet this remarkable economic achievement is being 'written out' of UK history by the neo-liberal academics of today.

So if Scotland is intending to establish a financial system which will blend with a Keynesian style economic policy then control of the currency and monitory policy is vital. In a later chapter we will examine some international examples which show the importance of this link between currency control and economic control giving some real life examples of how this vital link needs to be understood and controlled.

Currency Changes

It is also important to recognise that people do not like change, particularly when it will affect something close to them which is important to them, so any suggestion that the money in your pocket is going to be changed will create an automatic objection in people's minds which has to be overcome.

Of course in real life, currency changes all the time, both at the visible level and the invisible level. When the change is at the invisible level, like the change of some mutual building societies from full-reserve financial businesses, to fractional-reserve banks, most people did not notice the difference, so were not much concerned with it. However when the British currency was decimalised in 1971 people did take notice, indeed there were people expressing concern and fear about this in the media for months around this change.

Therefore we should make as few changes to the visible aspects of the new currency as we can, while changing the invisible aspects in order to secure the type of new currency we need.

We should announce that we will continue to use the pound for international trade but we will set-up a new Scottish National Bank, which like the Bank of England would be a nationalized bank. The new SNB would issue a new set of Scottish Pound notes, which it would be entirely responsible for. These new notes would be very similar to the current Scottish pound notes in appearance so no great change in the visible currency. However the new notes would be issued on a full-reserve currency basis and their supply would be strictly controlled by the SNB and they would initially be 'on a par' with the sterling exchange rate.

Scotland would need to bring in legislation which established the constitutional position of the Scottish currency and the regulations relating to banking in Scotland. As Scotland's currency would be established initially on a par with the pound sterling, it is obvious that if it was available for international exchange like the pound, it would offer currency speculators a great opportunity to acquire a full reserve currency in exchange for a fractional reserve currency, at no additional cost. This would lead to currency speculation, which could damage sterling and the new Scottish currency. So the new Scottish currency would be used for domestic exchange only, and the pound sterling would be used for international exchange.

There are of course a whole number of new ideas about currency and 'not-for-profit' banking which could be looked at as regards the new Scottish currency. One interesting view is that being put forward by the New Economic Foundation (NEF)* which is of considerable interest. Professor Nigel Dodd of the NEF is proposing a currency plan for Scotland now, as part of the UK and within the sterling system. His plan would see the Scottish Government setting up an account for all citizens over 18 who appear on the electoral register, with a free gift of £250 in it and using this to develop a Scottish currency.

There are some good ideas in their proposals, but it would work much better if it were used in an independent Scotland at the launch of a full-reserve Scottish pound.

The introduction of the Scottish pound should not be visibly significant for most Scots. While the change from fractional-reserve to full-reserve, would go unnoticed. The current arrangement for the Scottish pound is not significantly different from what I propose in Scotland. Scottish banks are allowed to print their own 'Scottish' notes. However they have to lodge pound for pound the full amount in pounds sterling in the Bank of England. This in essence is a full-reserve system within sterling. The only difference we are proposing is that only the SNB would print Scottish pounds in future and the 'reserve' for this currency would be held by the SNB and not the BoE.

Full Reserve Currency

Earlier, in the introduction we pointed out that currency is not wealth. It is merely a medium of exchange, which should not be confused with real wealth. One of the major problems we have in the world economy today is connected to currency and how it relates to the real economy and real wealth.

The term 'sterling' is derived from silver. In modern Gaelic we use the word 'airgiod' for money. Airgiod also means silver in Gaelic. This link between money, or currency and precious metals is not, of course, accidental. The promise to pay written on your five pound note originally referred to payment in silver or gold. But the UK 'came off the gold standard' in 1925. Which means that since then this promise to pay in silver or gold 'on demand' is no longer valid.

So what does the promise mean today?

To-day the Pound, the Dollar and the Euro are fiat currencies. This means that their value, which is in real commodities, is guaranteed by the State which issues the currency and nothing else. So the value of the pound today, which changes relative to other currencies from day to day up or down, really depends on what the UK state, can afford to give in real resources to redeem the promise.

Now, if the number of people wanting to acquire pounds is comparable with the number wanting to redeem them, there is no problem the exchange is in equilibrium, one balances out the other. Indeed if they are not equal, but not widely diverse, this can be adjusted by the international exchange rate between the currencies which operates on a daily basis.

For normal minor fluctuations, this system works fine; but of course it can't cope with any major fluctuation. In these circumstances the system could break down completely, it is the same as we saw with the banking system in 2008.

The problem comes not from normal trading, but when there is a general rise in demand from customers on different banks at the same time. Now we saw what happened then in the western world banking system. It started in the USA then rapidly spread to the UK then the EU. The banking system was collapsing everywhere. It was Gordon Brown and Alistair Darling who 'saved the world' with a great plan which took huge sums from the taxpayers and gave this to the private banks.

That brought a temporary settlement to the banking liquidity problem, but at huge cost to public expenditure and National Debt for the States who followed that policy. This was also accompanied by a desperate policy of austerity to 'pay back our public debts', which in turn damaged our real economy and countless people's lives.

This attempt to stabilise the pound did not end with the £billions given to them by the Government to save them from collapse, it has continued under the Government's Quantitative Ease (QE) programme. This is taken from the Keynesian idea of investing money into the economy in order to stimulate economic growth, which in turn will give you a return on that money in real terms. However, unlike the Keynesian plan QE does not work like the Keynesian model, and for very obvious reasons. A recent report* shows that QE in the UK resulted in £600 billion going to the rich while not one penny of it went to the 50% of the poorest people in the UK.

These measures however, are only designed to meet short term problems in the banking system they are not designed to be a long term solution to the fractional-reserve problem, they were merely a short-term relief.

The basic problem remains and will cause another collapse in the system it is merely a matter of time.

If therefore an independent Scotland can establish a full-reserve currency from the start, it can escape from this future problem and give our children and grandchildren a secure financial future. A full-reserve currency for Scotland could provide this and we must ensure that we establish such a currency.

Now the present Scottish banknotes in circulation, only amount to some 3% of the total money supply operating in Scotland today. However unlike the pound sterling they represent a full-reserve currency, because for every Scottish pound in circulation there is one 'full' pound sterling deposited in the BoE, not a 'fraction' of one. We believe that using the new Scottish National Bank (SNB) the reserves for our currency in circulation should be covered, as now, on a full pound for pound basis, but the reserve should be held in the SNB.

This currency should be expanded to cover all public expenditure from the Scottish Government on the same basis i.e. for every pound of public investment in the Scottish economy the SNB should hold Government assets to the same value. This would mean that the Scottish pound would be used in public investment in Scotland and would be expanded to meet its general circulation and public investment needs by assets held as reserves by the bank or as a record of public assets of the Scottish Government. In this way the objective of developing a full-reserve currency in Scotland could be introduced even indeed within the terms of a 'temporary agreement' with sterling. We should agree such an arrangement with the UK as part of any temporary agreement. If we do not have such an agreement with the UK Government then most certainly, we should develop a Scottish full-reserve currency.

Such a financial arrangement would give the Scottish Government control over its currency (which the UK does not have) and something else, interest free public investment money.

This would have the added value of meeting one of the other objections which the r-UK Government could have had about Scotland sharing sterling. It was claimed that if Scotland was sharing sterling and wanted to increase public expenditure at a time when the UK Government were reducing public expenditure this would put 'unfair' pressure on the pound. However if the Scottish Government's public investment policy was contained within its own fully funded Scottish pound the only limit on the Scottish Government's investment would be its ability to cover such investment with assets. This would have no adverse effect on the viability of the pound sterling. Indeed it would improve it, if the total volume of activity rose while the vulnerability element remained static. So even within a temporary sterling agreement this conversion to full-reserve currency could work, but outwith sterling it would have no difficulty.

If Scotland operated like Panama with its own currency internally but using sterling as an international currency, without any agreement, for international trade this would not present us with any particular problems, and after a period of time we could decide in the Scottish Parliament what our future currency arrangement were going to be and how this was reflected in our written constitution.

Let us be clear about this. If Scotland was using its own 'Scottish Pound' for domestic use and was using the pound sterling, on par, for international exchange this would not by itself cause any problem provided that everything remained the same. But of course, economics is a dynamic system, therefore by its nature things do not remain the same.

One thing very likely to change in a way which Scotland might not be happy with is the international value of the pound, and this might in time mean that an independent Scotland may want to devalue the Scottish Pound relative to the pound sterling for sound economic reasons.

Earlier on in this book when discussing Scottish Steel, I said that the steel company TATA had blamed the high pound as one of the reasons for the difficulty they had in selling UK steel. Now when Britain was a manufacturing country it was very aware of the danger of the pound having too high an exchange rate in comparison with other competing manufacturing countries. As you will appreciate if a currency is overvalued, relative to another it makes selling manufactured goods more expensive and less competitive.

As the UK has become less and less a manufacturing country and more and more depending on financial services there has been a tendency to keep pressure on maintaining a high value pound, rather than allowing the pound to settle at a lower rate. This has been helpful to the banks but not to UK manufacturers looking for markets abroad.

A new Scotland would need to have a good sound manufacturing base, it would have no economic interest in maintaining a high value Scottish Pound and there would be no private vested interest in the banking sector to do this. This could mean that the Scottish Government may have a different approach to the value of the Scottish pound, than the UK establishment had in relation to sterling.

The guiding principle on this, as indeed on other issues relating to currency is this. Always remember money has no intrinsic value, money's sole job in the economy is to serve the economy not to dominate it. So in relation to the real economy, real production always comes first, money is only there to serve. When you lose sight of that principle you get into trouble.

So let us be clear. If the UK Government is prepared to discuss with the Scottish Government a long-term agreement on trade, designed to help the r-UK with its national debt problem;we should be prepared to engage in this, on the clear understanding that there will be a post referendum short-term agreement on Scotland using sterling. However Scotland would not be involved, or 'share' responsible, for sterling. Any such agreement would need to be concluded before the independence referendum debate started.

If this is not agreed by the UK Government we must interpret this as a clear indication that they intend once again to use 'currency' in a repeat attempt to engage in another 'project fear' programme.

In such circumstances we must lay the facts bare for all to see. The UK Government has created the debt mountain it is their responsibility to resolve it and theirs alone. Scotland has no legal responsibility for any of this debt, or its servicing. Since the UK Government has rejected Scotland's offer to help, Scotland accepts this rejection with regret.

Scotland will use the Scottish pound within Scotland and the pound sterling in international trading following independence. Scotland will start its new independent economic life with no National Dept and with a full-reserve currency.

Now the Scottish Government must be entirely open with the people in explaining the advantages, and possible disadvantages of changing the currency arrangement. Indeed it is to The Scottish Government's advantage to do this and to do it very effectively because there are considerable advantages in this for Scotland and few disadvantages.

The big advantages are to get-out of a debt-crippled system which is currently costing each Scottish household £1,865 per annum (and rising). Also to allow the Scottish Government to have interest free public investment money. Also to ensure that all deposits in Scottish banks will belong entirely to the individual depositor and not as presently the case to the bank. (That is why we need guarantees from the bank which will give us some of our money back if the bank fails).

There are of course disadvantages, changes of this nature invariable cause short term disruption of the system and change in such things is never welcome; but we should face these challenges and compare them with the substantial gains.

What we must not do is allow people to insist they we should accurately predict the future and try to respond to that ridicules challenge. We can't predict the future, nor can anyone else, what we can do is look at huge amounts of debt which requires vast amounts of interest to service and we can then predict what needs to come out of our future earnings to pay that sum. That we can do. But we can't guarantee that the sun will continue to shine on the earth, empirically, that would seem likely, and it is reasonable to take such empirical evidence into account in our assessments, but, like everyone else, we can't guarantee that the sun will continue to rise every day we just have to rely on what physics predicts and the empirical evidence. We can't tell the future beyond our knowledge of science, however much our critics demand that we should.

*Matthew Sherman 'A Short History of Financial Deregulation in the UK' Center for Economic and Policy Research (CEPR) Washington

* Adam Smith 'An Inquiry into the Nature and Causes of the Wealth of Nations 1776 Edinburgh

* Joseph Stiglitz 'Freefall' 2010

* Angus Deaton 'The Great Escape'

* John Maynard Keynes 'The General Theory of Employment Interest and Money 1936

* New Economic Foundation Web-site

* Ripped off Britain Report 26-10-15

Chapter 4

Economic development

Many of us, undoubtedly the vast majority, will be seeking that from the independence campaign so it is wise for us to look now at the sort of economic policies which we will need to develop in such a new Scotland. If we do that and do it properly, then people will see that we know where we are going and how to get there, they are then more likely to come along with us.

As I indicated earlier the economic objectives set out in our book 'Moving On' were not widely different from the economic policies which the SNP Government wanted to pursue if they had the economic power, so let me start from there.

Let's take the objective of extending and developing wave power generation of electricity just as an example. Scotland has great potential for the development of this natural energy source. If it can be done in an effective industrial way it could be a major source of wealth to Scotland's future economy. In addition it would be a boost to employment, to research, to technology, to our exports, to our environment and to our world-wide reputation if we meet our anti global warming target.

Now Scotland has all the ingredients to make this possible, it has the political will and with political independence it will have the political authority all it will need then is the investment. Now let me make one thing clear here 'investment' in a real economic sense is not money. It is real resources labour, materials, equipment, tools etc; all of which can be express in terms of money. This 'investment' could come from a private source, or Government, or mixed government and private, or community source, it makes no difference in economic terms, however in new, high risk, industries Government investment is the surest way of getting the project started.

Now we all know, from experience, what the media will now ask. "Well where is the money going to come from?" The media belongs to the financial elite so they are hyper sensitive to financial investment. Many members of the public, who get most of their economic education from the media and are therefore practically economically illiterate, will ask the same question, because we have all been conditioned to believe that nothing positive can be done unless a rich patron helps us, for a wee consideration of course.

Well this is where we need to recognise that Government economic policy needs to be supported by Government power over currency and monetary policy. Where this is the case, like for example in Iceland, the answer is simple. "No problem we will have it printed". If on the other had the Government has political power, but no power over the currency like Greece the answer is not simple. "We don't know, we'll ask the private banks, or EU officials"

What if we were to ask a future Scottish Government, which had full economic and financial powers, such as suggested at option 1 or 2 above the same question? Where will the money come from? Then they would be able to say, like Iceland "No problem we'll have it printed".

A Scottish Government in that position would have no difficulty over public investment of that sort. It could get the full quantity of money it required, interest free, and still within its full-reserve currency system. Now some 'experts' will tell you that this would not work, that this printing money would cause inflation and ruin the money system. Well they are wrong, it can be done and indeed it has been done in Britain before and it can be again.

In addressing this it will be helpful if I take you through this and explain the situation, it is not complicated, but it may seem strange to those who have not come across it before.

The way it is done is the way Keynes did it, during the Attlee Government, and as he explains in his famous book 'The General Theory'*. If a Government has unemployment and natural resources, and if it controls money supply; it can employ these resources on public work projects and pay for the labour and the materials with the money it has printed. Once the work gets under way and before it becomes productive, the money paid in wages and for materials will start to get spent in the economy.

The 'new' money will circulate and 'multiply' as it circulates. For example, if £100 of new money is spent in the market it will be used again by the people who earned it and spent again. Now next time round the amount will be smaller say £80 but it will all happen again, next time perhaps £65 and so on. You can see how the Keynesian multiplier works. It is not 100% multiplication because money taken out for savings, or spent outside the economy (imports) would be lost in the next round. If we look at the graph in Keynesian Multiplier (1) we can see that this initial Government injection of £100 million in pound notes, creates around £500 million in 'real wealth'.

KEYNESIAN MULTIPLIER (1)

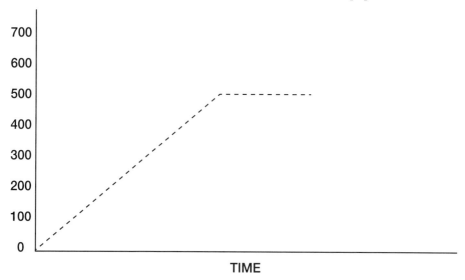

TIME

This simple explanation of the multiplier is very basic and leaves out a number of factors, one of the most important of which is the propensity to save (high among the wealthy; low among the poor). Also of course we need to find a low propensity to spend on imports. (Once again, this is high among the wealthy low among the poor) Now this, as you can imagine, can tell us that if we want to get a high multiplier working quickly then money injected into the hands of the poor will do a much better job than the same amount injected into the wealthy section of society. That is the main reason why inequality holds back demand and damages the economy.

But now back to our project. Now you have seen that even before the first wave power plant has produced one megawatt of power the printed money has started to multiply and is producing more economic activity which is now producing 'real wealth'. Now let us go over that again. The Government printed paper money (which is certainly not wealth) it paid this paper money to workers and suppliers and they spent it to purchase real goods and services, (which is real wealth); now this in turn was repeated, which means than more real wealth was created, this process is repeated a number of times. Therefore valueless paper money was exchanged for real wealth, which created more real wealth, to meet the new multiplying demand.

This all started to happen before the wave-energy plant was in operation. Once it is operating and in production it is now producing more real wealth and all this new real wealth is being covered by the production of new money to help it to circulate. The wealth is multiplied and the whole society is becoming wealthier, but it is not the money which is making them richer, money is merely being used like oil in an engine the real wealth is the new production which has been stimulated.

Now if that is clear to you, you will understand that an economic policy designed to work like that is not mysterious it is just common sense, but it uses money to suit the real economy not the other way round. It is worth taking note at this stage, that the Keynesian multiplier works on the way down just as well as on the way up, so Government cuts in public investment start the multiplier working downwards. In the following graph Keynesian Multiplier (2) we show the multiplier working downwards with the same figures turning a £100 million cut, into a £500 million reduction in real wealth.

KEYNESIAN MULTIPLIER (2)

TIME

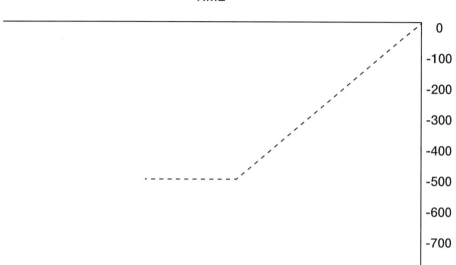

This multiplier effect is not magic, or mysterious, it is just the logical responses to a particular set of circumstances. When the multiplier is going up, in addition to the extra wealth produced the community now needs to spend less on unemployment benefits and other social welfare payments from the Government and the Government gets a higher tax take, which in effect gives the Government the original valueless money 'stake' back again.

Now that is an illustration of the Keynesian approach. But what about our full-reserve currency, did we not abandon that when the Government printed the money initially?

Well no, this did not challenge the full-reserve principal. Because the Government only agreed to release, let us say £100 million for the project in exchange for the asset i.e. the wave-power plant valued, of course, at £100 million. So while the government increased the money supply by £100 million it also increased its public assets by the same amount at the same time.

Now inflation is defined as too much money chasing too few goods forcing prices up. So it is true that if you increase money supply and do not increase goods or services, then this will cause inflation somewhere in the economy. (That indeed is where high house prices and land values come from). However if you increase goods and services, at the same time as you increase money, it does not have an inflationary effect.

So this proposal gives a clear answer to the question "where is the money coming from?

Now if the Government were to invest in wave-power production, it would make good sense to also invest in some other area of power creation if a suitable opportunity presented itself, because spreading the investment, spreads the risk and extends the opportunities.

The Scottish Government would perhaps be wise to do what the Norwegian Government did some years ago, and acquire a small oil company. Right now with oil prices low it should be possible for the Scottish Government to pick up a small oil company fairly cheaply. Norway acquired a small company like that in 1972, Norway nationalized it and developed it and it is now a major would wide company operating in 30 countries called Statoil.

It is in Scotland's interest to have a stake in the oil industry, as it was in Norway's interest to do so, for the simple reason that this natural resource needs to be carefully monitored in any country which has a significant amount of it.

So any country which wants to be able to develop its economy must ensure that it keeps tabs on its natural resources, its labour force and its currency. The link between an independent country and its currency is of great importance and we will look at that in the next chapter.

Domestic Currency

I explained in the previous chapter the need to establish a full-reserve currency in Scotland, for the domestic economy if we had no currency agreement with the UK Government. If however we did have such an agreement we would still need to organise our domestic currency in the same way and convert it into a full-reserve currency.

As we explained the instability in the fractional-reserve system is not confined to sterling, it affects the Dollar and the Euro as well. So while working in the international market using sterling we must take steps in the domestic market to establish a full-reserve currency which will protect the Scottish economy in the future when the Western Banks have another crisis.

The temporary agreement with sterling is not a reason to do nothing on the domestic currency situation, on the contrary, it is an opportunity to go ahead and make changes within the framework of the temporary sterling agreement. This agreement should be used to maintain our external market on the same basis as before, while we put in place all that is required to make a significant change to our domestic currency, while retaining parity with sterling and having very little visible change.

So while on the surface the currency situation might appear very much the same with no change. Major changes would need to be made under the surface. The New Scottish National Bank (SNB) would need to be established at the heart of the new currency system.

This would be a nationalized bank responsible to the Scottish Government, but its structure and control would be established in Scotland's written constitution. This would be required, because the SNB would have the responsibility for maintaining a full-reserve currency and for ensuring that the banking system as a whole in Scotland complied with banking laws and regulations established by the Scottish Parliament.

This would place the SNB in a significant position in relation to the other banks in Scotland. It would also mean that these banks would not be able to operate in the way they do today.

They could remain private banks, or be mutual society banks, or community banks or whatever; but they would be required to operate under tightly controlled regulations, which imposed on them a duty to operate on a full-reserve basis like a mutual society is required to do now. This may not be attractive to any of the present big four 'zombie' banks currently operating in Scotland, because they are bankrupt and need taxpayers help to survive.

This would change the banking system into a public service which had a responsibility to 'oil the wheels' of the economy. Such a standard banking system would not be designed to make profit for its shareholders. Its role would have to be much greater than that, it would be an essential part of the economic infrastructure of the country.

Some will tell us that this could lead to us 'losing' some of our big banks who would go elsewhere, to the city perhaps.

Well let us face this threat, or is it a promise; with open eyes.

RBS, which was once the largest bank in the world, but is now a 'zombie' bank and a huge liability, may want to leave Scotland. The UK Government owns most of it, not because they wanted to, but because it would have collapsed if they did not take it on. In an independent Scotland there will be no place for banks which depend for their survival on fractional reserve banking and the phantom money it can produce.

Banks and financial organisation which can't accept this will have no place in the new Scottish economy. This means that they will be required to adjust to operate on a more honest full-reserve system or not at all in Scotland. Now if that means that RBS will leave Scotland, then provided they take all their debts and liabilities with them they are free to go. They will be replaced, without difficulty, by banks which will operate within the new Scottish law. Many of their staff will find employment with the new, smaller Scottish banks and will therefore provide a much improved service to the Scottish people and very likely see a big improvement in their incomes and working conditions.

Preparing our domestic currency in this way will provide the Scottish people with an effective and secure banking system. The banks will not need to offer customers any guarantees that they will get a minimum amount back if the bank collapse, as the present banking system has to do. This will not be required, because under a full-reserve system all the money in a person's bank account will belong to that person, not to the bank, as it does in the current system. So with a full-reserve bank there is never a time when the bank can go bankrupt and allow the money in your account to disappear.

With full-reserve banking the money in your account remains yours, if the bank fails, it will still retain the full value of its deposits in assets. So every individual's deposits are covered and are safe. That is why a return to this system of finance is important for our future.

We also need a Government with the required financial tools to implement the ambitious investment strategy we need to meet our Keynesian economic plans, because this is the way we will move away from austerity to full employment and decent living standards.

Banking Reform – Merchant Banks

As I have advocated currency should be used as the 'oil' of the economy which is its proper function. If it is used for speculation by currency speculators it distorts the real economy and causes deep economic damage. So the Scottish pound must be protected from such speculation in order to perform its job effectively and to be a long-term stable unit of exchange. While Scotland remains in the temporary sterling agreement its international trade can be conducted through the SNB in sterling. When Scotland leaves the temporary agreement with sterling other arrangement can easily be made for international exchange which would avoid currency speculation.

This is an area which is changing rapidly, a few years ago there was little option in international exchange arrangement which were not centred on the Dollar, or currencies such as the Pound or Euro linked to the Dollar.

This is going through major change at the moment with China, acting on behalf of the BRICs group of countries launching a new international exchange system offering an alternative, which the USA opposes, but which the UK has joined.

It is clear that the other banks in Scotland would need to be subject to major reform and would need to comply with regulations under the SNB supervision, there will be no room in the new standard Scottish banking system for speculation of the type we are familiar with, where banker's use other people's money to gamble with and keep the gains that accrue, but pass on any losses to others.

There will of course, be room for Merchant Banks, banks which would be able to provide a service for venture capital. Merchant banks could continue to operate in Scotland, but such banking must be separate from the standard banking system and would be subject to separate regulation. For example; it would be useful for merchant banks to offer loans to companies or individuals looking for capital to establish a new, or expanded business, and to do so at higher interest rates to meet the risk involved.

Now there are people who would be willing to commit funds from their savings to such merchant banks if they were offering higher interest to account for risk of loss. If one is prepared to place one's savings at risk by depositing them in a merchant bank on the promise that you are likely to get a higher rate of interest. Then many of us may be prepared to take that chance.

Indeed banks with a local bank manager who could interview whose looking for capital investment and, if satisfied with their business plan as likely to succeed in that area, make a decision to grant a loan on defined conditions. Such, old style banking, would be an asset to our economy. However such an arrangement should be financed by people who are aware of the risk and who are prepared to accept this for the possible rewards.

While this is, and should be legitimate. It should not be permitted within the standard banking arrangement where there is no specific agreement for deposits to be used for risk taking, and rewards for such risk taking are taken by a few people who risked other people's money. That system, which currently operates is totally unfair and unacceptable. If people are prepared to put their own money at risk, on the judgement of the bank manager; then they know that they could lose the money they have invested. If however there are higher rewards available as a result of this investment then they are entitled to their fair share of the rewards also.

There is little doubt that banks which wanted to concentrate on this area of business and who designed their organisation and trained their staff to meet this particular financial service; would be a great asset to the economy. Indeed the extent to which they made the right assessments and judgements would, over time, determine their ability to attract deposits. So their success would reflect background economic success for the people who borrowed from them. This type of banking activity would add to successful banking in Scotland, but it must never again be linked into the standard banking system, it must stand alone on its merits.

Savings and Investment.

Of course, people will point out to us that we can't have a full-reserve currency if we do not have savings. The idea of a full-reserve currency is that I can only invest with your money, if you are saving and not spending it. It is a system where money which is not being spent by 'a' can be spent by 'b'. So unless there are a sufficient number of people in Scotland prepared to put money into savings, then there will not be resources available for investment if the economy is at full capacity.

We need to be satisfied that we can be sure of a steady flow of savings over a long period at a level high enough to provide the relatively high investment levels we need, if we are to be sure that our system will work.

Fortunately we have years of experience and considerable data from the mutual building societies which operated in Scotland for many years. As indicated earlier we know that such societies did find the funding for the entire private housing stock in the UK, and did so from the savings of UK residents, so there is a prima facie case for being convinced that such savings would be available.

What evidence is there for this in Scotland now? That is a more difficult question to answer. In recent years savers have been getting virtually nothing in interest rates for their savings from the bank, because banks, with their phantom money do not require customer's savings and are not particularly interested in them.

However, all the evidence seems to show that many people, and many Scots in particular are still putting a considerable % of their earnings into savings, the 'This is Money co.uk' web-site* gives figures for saving by different groups, in different parts of the UK, which was updated in March 2013. This survey shows that Scotland has the second highest level of savers, in the whole of the UK, at £103 per capita per month; or 8% of income.

Now considering that people are not getting anything by the way of interest on their savings, this shows a remarkably high level of savings in a period of major austerity.

It is clear that this level of savings would meet the requirement for fairly high sustained investment, and clearly if better interest were offered this could raise the amount of savings available.

Scottish Government Preparations.

The Scottish Government needs to put more energy and consideration into the relationship between finance and the economy. It was evident to some of us that we went into the referendum debate last time, quite unprepared to deal with the currency/economy issue, and it turned out to be the SNP's greatest mistake in the campaign.

On the whole the SNP Government did extremely well in the campaign, to have raised the profile of independence in the way that it did, and to have engendered the huge involvement of people as it did was very impressive. Few serious people now doubt that Scotland is moving towards an independent future.

However, we have to make our own history, we can never be complacent and assume that things will continue to move in the direction we want them to do. We have to now take the view that only a clear win in any future referendum is acceptable, therefore we need to take a positive hand in events if we want to direct the outcome. The Scottish Government now needs to examine and carefully review its policy on currency long before we get into the pre-referendum debate.

Of course, in the real world, as in the world of economics, constant change and development is the norm. So any moves we are contemplating needs to be in line with movements elsewhere. So some understanding of what is happening in the wider world is important if we want to adopt an economic stance in the future which is likely to become more relevant over time.

The SNP have done this quite successfully in the recent past by adopting an anti-austerity position. It is increasingly clear that not only was that stance popular with Scottish people, but it was becoming increasingly popular with people all over Europe. Even in England the effects of an anti-austerity stance on the Labour leadership was dramatic as we have noted.

The SNP did select this particular 'social wave' at an early point and are currently at the crest of this wave; however they need to ride it successfully or they will mess-up and go under. We have seen how the ruling establishment has faced this social wave so far, we saw it quite openly in Greece. They have no way of meeting this popular demand and they have no alternative to their 'austerity' policies which are failing; so we must stay on this wave right through to independence.

The lesson is clear. Currency was used in Greece to force the people into acceptance of 'austerity' against their democratic will. We all saw it played out. It appears on the surface to have won, just as project fear appeared to have won in Scotland; but in reality neither of these have won the war, they have merely won the first battle. The pressure from people will continue to build. The lesson for politicians is clear, if you take on austerity, you take on the ruling elite and their fractional-reserve banking system. Greek politicians lost the first round, because they did not face it with a realistic plan. Jeremy Corbyn will fail in England because he has not got an economic plan which can over-ride the banking elite in the city.

Scottish politicians should have been reading the signs. The SNP economic policy can succeed but only if it can effectively address the financial aspect. It must be obvious to anyone who gives it consideration, Scotland, politically independent or not, can't put in the level of public investment it needs to turn round the Scottish economy unless it can resolve the finance issue. Sticking your head in the sand and refusing to look, is never a valid policy.

There is absolutely no point in politicians having a first class economic policy which will address all the problems of unemployment, low productivity, low incomes, inequality, dire poverty, lack of opportunity and many other adverse effects of a failing economy; unless and until they have the means to ensure that their policies can be implemented.

The Greek Government had a sound economic policy; it was a Keynesian policy of the type employed by the Attlee Government in post war Britain. Their policy was not unlike the SNP Scottish Government policy; but neither of them can implement their policies.

Neither the Greek Government, who have political independence, but no economic independence; nor the Scottish Government, who have no political independence nor enough economic independence, can implement their economic policies. This should make it clear to us that political independence, but still restricted within sterling, would not allow Scotland to have the economic power it requires to implement its policies.

What Greece lacked was a financial policy, which could be used to implement their economic policy. They were depending on others in the EU, Germany in particular, to provide the financial basis for their economic policy and we know what happened to that.

We must ensure we recognise the vital importance of having an effective financial system which can act effectively to 'oil the wheels' of the economy. There is little point in constructing a first class, well engineered car engine and trying to test it in a race if we have no oil to put in it. No matter how good the engine is, it will fail. A first class expensive engine will be ruined for the cost of a cheap can of oil.

The economy is the same. Building an effective and well balanced economy with the right supply of natural resources to blend with the labour, education and skills mix is like building a well designed engine. Given the right fuel, which in this case is natural resources, all we need is oil to ensure that the performance will be first class. If however someone else has control of the oil can this needs to be addressed before we run the engine.

The Scottish Government has sensibly made it clear that they would not wish to arrange a campaign for another referendum on Scottish Independence unless and until there were demands for this from the people and valid reasons for it. There could be no more valid reason I imagine than the fact that the UK Government are destroying the Scottish economy by austerity.

The Cameron Government has a small Westminster majority and seems hell bent on driving the austerity policy full pelt. The outcome of this stupidity it not difficult to predict; either this Government will be brought down by its own economic failures, or the UK economy will suffer another major decline. If you have no manufacturing base, and few natural resources and you are deliberately driving down incomes; then you will drive down domestic demand.

It should be obvious that if you can't increase exports, because you do not have any, then high house prices in London, although it may help the GDP to look like its rising, will not save the real economy from actual falls in real economic values. Once it becomes obvious, that if you have reduces demand by £Billions more among the lowest income groups in society therefore the people with the highest propensity to spend, the 'Keynesian' multiplier will drive down demand.

This can only have one outcome 'real' income for the vast majority of people in the UK will fall. The only way this can be prevented is by massive investment in productive industry and services, which with a devaluation of the pound could enable a major rise in exports; in other words because demand in the UK is falling the only way to raise production is to find demand from abroad.

However that is not the way the present UK Tory Government is heading, indeed they are driving full-speed in the opposite direction. They have actually swallowed their own neo-liberal propaganda and believe that the slight increase in the GDP which they have seen 'proves' that the UK economy is about to grow. The sad truth is that this 'growth' they are so impressed with is no more than a rise in prices, mainly property prices and luxury goods. It is not a growth in goods or productive investment. Manufacturing and construction are falling as is productivity in this so called recovery.

Napoleon is alleged to have told one of his officers before a battle that it was clear that the enemy were making a mistake. "What do you plan to do then" the officer asked him "I don't plan to do anything" he replied, "If your enemy is busy making a mistake, don't interrupt him" he said.

It may be that in this particular struggle we should take Napoleon's advice. If Cameron and Osborne are busy making a mistake, we should take note of their position and plan our strategy with that in mind

This was undoubtedly the thinking in William Wallace's mind in 1297, as he watched the English army cross Stirling Bridge in their thousands and line up on a piece of marshy ground and a causeway. He could see that they were making a huge mistake which was putting them in real danger from his small army. He did not however show his hand, he waited patiently for hours until they had deployed nearly half of their huge army into that trap, then he sprung the trap.

The lesson I believe is, that in any struggle between two sides, on the battlefield, or playing-field, or political arena; we have to observe how our opponent is playing before we can determine our own final tactics.

We can now see the opposition's full hand all their cards are on the table. We would be very foolish therefore not to read their strategy and devise a way of countering it which leads towards our objectives.

Now, just like Surrey and Cressingham, the English Commanders at Stirling Bridge, Cameron and Osborne are making the same mistake; they have no respect for their opponents. This is dangerous, because it leaves you very vulnerable to attacks you are ill prepared for.

It seems to me, as an observer that their arrogance is leading them into making exactly the same mistake. They are sure of themselves having beaten the Scots at the referendum and having since that routed their 'main' enemy the Labour Party at the GE. They do not see that they are now moving their main force onto 'marshy' ground.

By driving down incomes for families in the low-income groups, they will in fact undermine the 'economic' ground they are standing on. They have not yet seen this and are still arrogantly and aggressively pursuing their austerity policy and condemning all who disagree.

It is clear that the best political position for us to adopt is to confirm our total opposition to austerity and put forward a solid and sensible way out of the economic mess. If we do that and are seen by others to have found solid ground and to have a clear way out of the bog then people will come over to our side and support us. Particularly as the water level starts rising and those in the bog start sinking.

So we should enter this next battle in the war with quiet confidence, but we must face economic reality. We must examine carefully the economic way forward for the Scottish economy. The economic way forward which the SNP Government is currently pursuing is fundamentally correct and has already attracted great support in Scotland. We therefore have the engine design, but we must not forget the 'oil' this time. We need a clear and simple view on currency for the new Scotland, in order to ensure we have the oil for this engine.

If we can understand and, at the right time, advance boldly and confidently into the attack then we stand on the threshold of an historic advance for the Scottish people and for humanity in general. With the help of Cameron and Osborne it will not be long before we go into another battle. If it is well planned, it should be like a Stirling Bridge encounter for us.

In the next chapter I will explore the relationship between currency and economic activity in different small countries in order to try and show the importance of the relationship between Government control of its own currency and its control of the economy.

- John Maynard Keynes 'The General Theory of Employment, Interest. and Money'
- www.This is Money.uk web-site

Chapter 5

International Comparisons

If we want to look at this issue objectively from a Scottish point of view we need to ignore the UK establishment and media, because you can't get an unbiased view from that source. It is equally true of course, that you will not get an unbiased view from me, because I am committed to Scottish independence; but I do not pretend to be neutral and unbiased, my position is clear and up front. I will however work hard to be objective, in the sense that I will look at the objective facts. Of course, I will see the positive side clearly, but may not always put enough focus on the negative side. You will need to judge that for yourself. The only way to make objective judgements in a situation like this is to look for similar, but unrelated comparisons. I will try in this chapter to help you with this.

If we pick a number of countries with which we want to compare Scotland, we must find countries with some basic similarities, so that the comparisons are reasonable. I have chosen three other countries, all of which have some basic similarities, but have differences in the relationship between Government control over finance and the economy in general, which is of course the comparison I want to make.

The countries I have chosen are Iceland, Panama and Greece, in that order; because Iceland is an independent country, outwith the EU, which has its own currency and has direct control of its own economy.

Panama is politically independent although it is under strong US 'influence'; it has its own internal currency, but uses the Dollar (without any agreed arrangement) for its external trade. It has control of its domestic economy and a reasonable international trading relationship.

Finally, I will consider Greece, which has political independence, but does not have its own currency and has no control over currency, in the domestic economy or in international trade. So if we group these countries, in that particular order we go from the most economically independent with the most economic control both internally and internationally, to the country with least control. Scotland of course, which is still like a colony, has neither political independence nor economic independence at the moment.

If Scotland is aspiring to independence what particular model should it see as the most appropriate of the three examples I have selected.

Of course, you may not think that these examples are the best and that there are more appropriate examples, that may be so, I can't think of any more appropriate but there may well be. The important thing however is to examine alternative examples, if it does not help you, it will most certainly not harm you to do so.

I have chosen these because they are all small countries. You will note that being a small country is often claimed by opponents of Scottish independence as being a negative factor for Scotland in its quest for independence. Well all the examples I have chosen are smaller than Scotland except Greece and Greece is the least economically successful of the 4 countries. So I believe that size is not a handicap for a country's economic development. I could have switched Iceland for Norway in the above list because both would fit this category, but Iceland is much smaller than Scotland, so it illustrates this additional point.

The other similarity is that all these countries, in my lifetime have been under the control of larger states. So the people in these countries know what it is like to have a 'big brother' looking after your economy for you. So I will give a short history of each country's struggle for independence and the circumstances under which they achieved their political independence because that also has relevance to their present situation.

In terms of natural resources only Iceland has rich natural resources comparable with Scotland, but we could consider the Panama Canal as comparable with a natural resource as far as the Panama economy is concerned. However as regards the range of natural resources Scotland is in a more powerful position than any of the others in these groups and indeed of most small countries internationally.

Iceland

Iceland is a very small country with a population of only around 323,000, about the size of Edinburgh. Iceland has however a long history of fighting to secure its independence, like Scotland in that respect. Also like Scotland Iceland has a very early history of literature in the Latin script form. The Viking Saga's all originated in Iceland where the early Norse language was converted into Latin Script. It is indeed likely that this early development of writing in Iceland was assisted by Scot's or possibly Irish monks who inhabited Iceland before the Vikings got there. The Irish Gaelic language was the first northern European language to adopt the Latin Script, and it is known that monks using that language had a presence in Iceland when the Vikings arrived.

Iceland struggled, unsuccessfully most of the time, to maintain its political independence for many centuries this is well recorded in history. Finally in 1944 when the Nazi occupation was ended, Iceland became an independent state and has remained firmly in that position since then. It is perhaps important that Iceland was not threatened, or overshadowed by the powerful state which had dominated it before it became independent. The Nazi regime was crushed completely shortly after Iceland won its independence so Iceland was not threatened by Germany, or Denmark or any other state in post war Europe and so it did not have to bend to the influence of a larger more powerful neighbour in order to keep its independence.

Now the idea that because it is a tiny country with no standing army it can be pushed around and dictated to by stronger states has been demonstrated by Iceland to be invalid.

In 1958, and again in 1976 Iceland was involved in two 'cod wars' with the UK. The UK, compared to Iceland was a supper-state. It was a member of the UN Security Council; it had large forces, including one of the most powerful navies in the world, with nuclear weapons and a large air-force. The central issue was considered by Iceland to be in its vital economic interests. As an ex-whaling nation and a nation highly dependent on its own rich fishing areas; Iceland wanted to have a 12 mile territorial waters limit accepted internationally around Iceland.

The UK would not accept that and in typical UK negotiating style it threatened tiny Iceland with naval power, rather than negotiations. When the UK advised its fishing trawlers to fish within the limits of these new Icelandic territorial waters, the Icelandic customs craft moved around the trawlers and cut their trawling gear. The UK responded by sending in large naval ships to harass the Icelandic coastguard vessels and this cutting gear and naval harassment went on for some months. However Iceland stood their ground and won both encounters and most significantly won their 12 mile territorial waters claim which they still hold.

This fierce independence and defence of their own vital economic interests was displayed again by Iceland in the aftermath of the 2008 banking crisis. This particular example might be more relevant to the subject of this book.

Iceland, like most Western countries prior to 2008 was heavily engaged in the financial expansion of the fractional-reserve banking system with all its problems, however in relation to its size Iceland's banks created a massive problem for the country. In the years just before the 2008 bank crash Iceland's three largest banks Kaupthing, Landsbanki and Glitnir were rapidly multiplying in size on the expansion of phantom money in the fractional-reserve system, so at the time of the crash they had liabilities more than 10 times Iceland's GDP.

You could say that, on a per capita basis, Iceland was hit worse by the banking crisis than any other country.

Iceland's response however was very different. They did not respond to the Gordon Brown and Alistair Darling plan, which was to 'save the world' by using tax-payer money to bail-out the private banks.

They looked first to their own citizens and ensured that they had the guaranteed minimum which they were entitled to from their bank account and then forced the banks which were bankrupt to close down and founded new, smaller ones, to replace them. The British and Dutch banks had been closely linked with the big Icelandic banks and both these countries wanted Iceland to act differently. They wanted Iceland to bail out the banks with taxpayer's money, and they got involved in a dispute with Iceland about this. You can see some of the bitterness in this dispute if you look for the You-Tube video of Jeremy Paxman interviewing the Icelandic President Mr Olafur Ragnar Grimsson (6th Jan 2010)*

In this video Paxman behaves in an appalling way towards a head of state, he speaks to Mr Grimsson like he was a naughty school boy who has been misbehaving. It is an incredible video which is well worth watching. It tells us a great deal more about the link between the UK media and the Capitalist elite, than it tells us about the real financial issue; because the real issue is not discussed, just the demand that Iceland fall into line and support the big banks. Iceland's people and their independence and democracy is treated with contempt while Paxman shouts "Don't trust an Icelander" at the President.

Let us in a more intelligent way examine the way Iceland reacted to this banking crisis, which was indeed different from the way that all the other Western countries, who were directly involved, behaved.

Iceland saw the banks and those who ran them as responsible for this crisis. They adopted a position which would first ensure that their citizens got their maximum guarantee from the banks then closed these banks down and took legal action which finally led to many bankers going to prison. Their position was clear. These banks had been ignoring the regulations and breaking the law, and their activities had cause great damage to people and to the economy of the country. Therefore the businesses which were bankrupt should be closed down like any other business in that position, and those who were responsible for breaking the law must face the consequences of their actions and be punished by the law.

So what is so wrong with that? Is that not what a democracy working under the rule of law must do if it is to operate fairly in the service of its citizens?

The Paxman attack on the very idea that Iceland had the right, and the audacity to challenge what Brown and Darling were claiming was essential to save the world, shows the pressure Iceland came under in the attempt of big capital's ruling elite, to force every Government in every country in the Western World to get in line and support the banks with a taxpayer's bailout. In this recorded interview Paxman claims that the International Debt Assessment Agencies, the IMF, the EU and international 'opinion' were all convinced that in following the course it was on; Iceland's economy and international trade would be destroyed beyond recovery.

It may be that it was this 'pressure' which brought so many politicians from so many countries into line and agreeing to get their own people to pay for the banking crisis and to implement the recommended course of medicine 'austerity'.

But tiny Iceland's independence and confidence was too strong for this pressure and they stuck to their policy of sorting this banking mess out in accordance with the rule of law and in line with policy decisions made by the Icelandic people.

We now know, at the beginning of 2016, that Iceland was absolutely correct. Not only did all the dire warnings from Alistair Darling turn out to be groundless; but after the initial major shock to the Icelandic economy, it recovered faster than anywhere else in Europe. Of course Iceland's economy was initially hit hard by the banking crisis. In the first year it caused, the GDP to shrink by 6.8%, unemployment to rise significantly and the value of the Icelandic Króna to fall dramatically. However, the very fact that Iceland had its own currency which could absorb much of this economic shock, gave Iceland the chance to rebound with a vigorous economic recovery. Iceland's international trade has developed a pace, unemployment has fallen and its account with the IMF has greatly improved.

As for its international relations, it has withdrawn its request to join the EU, not because it could not get entry, but probably because as a member of the European Free Trade Association (EFTA) it felt that it had the trading relationship it needed with other European countries and did not require a political union. There are many in the UK who would like to see the UK in that position in its relationship with the EU.

The lesson from Iceland's history, including its current history, challenges the claim that small countries can't look after their people's vital interests in the modern world of super states. Iceland has taken its own road; in the teeth of opposition from large states, and has emerged stronger and more resilient than many large states have been shown to be.

What is however beyond doubt is that in this banking issue Iceland's greatest strength was that it had its own currency and was not dependent, like Greece for example, on others outside Iceland to support its financial policy. If Iceland had been in that situation, it would not have found the outside support which it would have required.

Panama

Now I want to move across the Atlantic to consider Panama.

Again Panama is a small country with a current population of around 3.7 million.

It became politically independent from Colombia in 1903 under the sponsorship of the USA, but many saw that as a move by the USA to get control of the Panama Canal project and their need for a local friendly administration in the canal region.

US influence has therefore always been in the background of the early development of Panama and this is very much reflected in every aspect of its economy. The largest and central issue was of course the construction and later control of the Panama Canal, which is undoubtedly the reason for US long-term interest in Panama.

In 1940 the Panamanian Government under President Arias replaced the Colombian peso, which had been the unit of currency with the Panamanian balboa, and then in 1941 he printed balboa notes for circulation.

The Americans did not like that, because these notes which were equivalent to 1.1 per Dollar could have given the Panamanian Government more control over its internal and external finances; so they put pressure on the Arias Government and the notes were withdrawn days later. These notes are known as the "Seven day Dollar" notes.

From the beginning in 1903 Panama was a Constitutional Democracy, but it operated in effect very much like a commercially orientated oligarchy. During the 1950's the Panamanian military began to challenge the oligarchy's political hegemony.

In the General Election on October 1st 1968 Dr Arnulfo Arias Madrid was elected President. The army ousted the president on the 11th of October 1968 and took over. US influence was not contend with its position in the background and was prepared to discard 'democracy' in order to make its influence more effective.

US influence moved from background to up front 21 years later, in December 1989, when the US invaded Panama, (condemned by the UN with the US, UK and France exercising their veto,) and removed the then political leadership of Manuel Noriega and established a new 'democracy' but of course, one under US influence and advice.

So although Panama can be classed as an independent country, it does not have the independence which Iceland could display. Its independence has to be within a range acceptable to the USA which takes a close interest in Panama's affairs.

While Panama has its own currency, the Balboa, we are aware that it is kept in restraint by the US. However Panama uses the balboa for the domestic economy, over which it has control through the state owned National Bank of Panama so the Government has some control in the banking sector, but Panama has been seen for many years as the Switzerland of the Americas, and has a reputation for light regulation and secrecy in international account handling.

Panama uses the dollar in international trade, and also to some extent internally. Panama's international trading is dominated by two significant factors the Panama Canal and the Colón Free Trade Zone which is the largest free trade zone in Latin America and handles around 92% of exports and 64% of imports for Panama*.

Panama's economic growth is described as the best managed in Latin America and with an unemployment rate of only 2.7% it has a good economic record. It is a significant economy in Latin America and for its size it 'punches well above it weight' in world economic terms.

The level of inequality is very bad, which has not in the past been unusual in Mid- and South- America. While many in the country are extremely wealthy there are very many living in dire poverty in 'third world' conditions.

Therefore compared with Iceland, Panama's independence is considerably restricted and was over-run completely in 1989 by invasion. Panama does have its own currency controlled by a state owned bank for the domestic economy, but the dollar is still used in the domestic economy and is used for the external economy. Panama can be seen as a sort of half way house between independent Icelandic control, and dependent Greek control which we will look at now.

Greece

This leads us to Greece the largest of the small countries for our consideration. Greece has a population of around 11 million so it is more than twice the size of Scotland.

Greece is also an 'independent' country and its struggle to maintain independence was also interrupted by the Nazis. The situation in Greece was different and involved the British in a less than reputable way.

When the Greeks freed themselves for the Nazis in 1944, which they had achieved with British help including the active assistance of some famous Scots soldiers, Churchill ordered the British army to turn on the Greek partisans, who had been allies in the fight against the Nazis. This happened only six weeks after the defeat of the Nazis in Athens and while the Greek people were still celebrating their victory over fascism.

Churchill had been given the right by the Churchill, Roosevelt, Stalin agreement to determine the future of Greece while Stalin was given the right to determine Poland's fate.

As a result of that understanding Churchill had decided that the Greek Partisans were too powerful and too sympathetic to communism for his liking, much as Stalin decided that the Polish partisans were too powerful to play a significant role in post war Poland. Churchill wanted the Greek King to be returned to Greece and a more right-wing Government to be installed, so he instigated a civil war in Greece. The British Imperialist love of 'divide and rule' so familiar with Churchill and his class was used by Churchill to exploit the divisions which existed between the partisans and the Nazi collaborators. He even supplied weapons to ex-Nazi collaborators.

Churchill's plan was to bring back the king and install a right-wing, anti-communist Government which would a-line itself with the UK and the USA. This activity was supported by British troops, who now turned on their war time allies in the partisans to support their old Nazi supporting enemies. This friction resulted in the massive civil war in Greece 1946 – 49 with much death and destruction. The success of Churchill's policy here was no victory for the Greek people. Later of course Greece lost its democracy. The very political idea which ancient Greece had given to Western Philosophy, to be ruled by military dictators linked to the USA.

This whole business in Greece is one of Britain's most shameful activities in its long sordid imperial legacy which we have inherited. It is no surprise that older Greek people will find it hard to expect any help for their country from Britain.

This means however that Greek independence which has existed 'on paper' since 1944 has had no real life until quite recent years. Its independence has emerged from blood and violence inflicted by the fascist sympathising thugs we gave support to in their oppression of the Greek people.

It is hardly surprising that with that post-war history Greek society and the Greek economy has not been particularly successful. However since the turn of the century the Greek economy was developing greater than average in the EU, its GDP reflected this. Greece joined the Euro in 2001 and abandoned its own currency.

Greece was hit hard by the banking crisis but even after years of economic decline it was still the 13th largest EU economy out of the 28 member countries in 2013. 81% of the Greek GDP comes under services but this includes Shipping which by itself accounts for 6.7% of GDP and the tourist sector which is substantial. The Greek merchant navy is the largest in Europe. With shipping such a large part of the Greek economy, much of it operating on an international basis the question of domestic taxation is a problem for the Greek Government.

Greece has a small but significant industrial base, around 16% GDP and a good agricultural base 3.4% GDP. However the banking crash has had a devastating effect on the Greek economy, on employment and living standards and the whole world has seen how austerity, forcing the Keynesian multiplier into reverse, has destroyed the lives of hundreds of thousands of the Greek people.

Whatever is the cause of the 'debt' problem, and that is wide open to interpretation, what is beyond doubt is that the austerity 'cure' is far worse than the illness. Unemployment, particularly among the young, is a disaster for any economy and anyone who attempts to justify it on economic grounds is either economically illiterate, a fool, or a crook.

Anyone can see that unemployment reduces the goods and services being created so it can't by itself help economic growth, now if it is a result of moving from one form of production to another it may have a medium-term purpose; however long-term unemployment can never be justified on economic terms.

If we look at what has happened to the Greek economy we can see immediately what the problem is: instead of currency being merely the oil which serves the engine of the economy, the economy is being adjusted to meet the requirements of the currency. That is ridicules and can't be justified in economic terms, and more importantly it will not work.

Now let us look at what the situation may have been if Greece had not joined the Euro in 2001. When the bank crisis happened they would have been hit like every other country, but certainly less so than Iceland, because of the ratio between banking as a % of their GDP.

They would, like most countries in Europe, have seen trade levels falling and this would have affected their economic activity. In those circumstances, and particularly if they had bailed out the banks with taxpayers money, as most of European countries did, then their national debt would have risen and the value of their drachma would have fallen, just as the value of the Icelandic Króna did at that time.

Now how would this fall in the value of the drachma have affected the economy? Imports into Greece would have risen in price, so those Greeks buying expensive German cars would have had to pay a lot more for them. On the other hand exports would have become cheaper so Greek shipping and Greek holidays would have become cheaper.

It would have had another effect, Greek demand for German cars as we have seen would have fallen, but Volkswagen the German car manufacturer would be looking hard at Greece as a place to build a new car plant, because the cost of production in Greece would be lower because of the low value of the drachma. So is would encourage inward flow of industrial investment to Greece which would help the Greek economy.

Therefore had Greece still been using the drachma, in its domestic economy the banking crash would have hit them like everyone else, but their recovery from it would have been much faster, because the currency would have been adjusted to meet the needs of the economy and not the other way round. A change in international value of a currency does not have any effect between real commodities within the domestic economy, the change only effects international exchange.

We may remember Harold Wilson's comments when the pound was devalued he said that "the pound in your pocket has not changed". Well Wilson was condemned for that statement on the basis that it was untrue, but it was after all, more than half true.

If the currency is devalued it has no effect on the bulk of economic exchanges which are between buyers and sellers in the domestic market. The change it has is when the buyer, or seller, is abroad, or using another currency. If I am buying eggs from a croft along the road at £1 a half dozen and the pound is devalued it makes no difference to the trading deal between us, I still give him a pound and he gives me a half-dozen eggs. Of course if he buys his chicken food from abroad he will have to pay more for it and it will gradually move into the domestic market in that way. It is however a double edged sword because imports are dearer while export are cheaper.

So the problem that Greece has, is not that it has a large national debt, (which country in Europe hasn't), nor that it has no resources, human and material to make wealth; the problem is that it is trying to do something which is not economically possible, to make the economy 'fit' the requirements of the currency; when it should be adjusting the currency to 'fit' the requirements of the economy.

Further International comparisons.

So what lessons can we draw from these international comparisons? Let me give one more international comparison with Scotland which might help with this.

One of the growing sources of income for Iceland is aluminium production. Iceland has 3 aluminium smelters employing around 1,400 and has become very efficient in world market terms at producing aluminium at a low market price. Now the main reason for that is because aluminium production is a high energy-intensive process; so low energy and transport cost are vital if you want to succeed in aluminium production. If you can get access to cheap energy, and have easy access to cheap transport links, then you can easily compete with people who have to pay high, or average, energy prices.

Now Scotland also still has a small aluminium smelter at Kinlochleven in Lochaber. The reason why an industrial process like this was built in the heart of the Highlands was precisely because it was next to the highest mountains in Britain and next to a sea loch. It got cheap electricity from its own hydro-power generated from water running down the mountain, and it was on the shore of a sea loch which could transport it's imputes and products all over Britain and overseas.

One can see the economic sense in this. Iceland with geo-thermal energy and deep sea lochs can obviously gain the same economic advantages and is currently exploiting that advantage.

Britain used to have 20,000 people producing aluminium worth £3 billion pounds per annum, a product which is in increasing demand not least because it is considered a very 'green' material for use, particularly in transport. However British Aluminium has merged with what is now Rio Tinto Alcan (Canada) and its plants at Lynemouth which used to produce 178,000 tonnes a year and Anglesey which produced 145,000 tonnes per year have now been closed with only the small Lochaber plant, 43,000 tonnes per year remaining.

Scotland, on the other hand, with the same economical advantages as Iceland, is fighting to save its aluminium smelter in Kinlochleven, and the 174 jobs there. Scotland still has the natural resources, the knowledge, the skill base and the workforce to make aluminium in competition with Iceland's efficient production system.

So if we lose this final production process in Britain for a material which Britain needs to import now, it can't be said that it was lost for economic reasons, because there are no economic grounds for destroying this industry in Scotland. This plant, and this industry could, and should have a bright future in Scotland, but we need to have a Scottish Government with the economic power to assist and support this industry and enable it to take full advantage of its location and natural resources, so that it can effectively exploit the market on its doorstep.

This Scottish Industry is in trouble because it is not getting the consideration it needs yet it had been placed in the Highlands in the first place, to take advantage of cheap electricity and low transport cost which it still has. The company's other plants in England and Wales may well have been in difficulty because of high energy costs, but this should not be the case in Lochaber. This was the very reason why the smelter was built there.

It makes no economic sense to treat this Scottish aluminium plant in the same way as the English and Welsh plants were treated in the UK, because the economic circumstances are quite different. However to a London centric Government a small industry with a few jobs is of little relevance, compared with their other priorities. In Lochaber 174, well paid, jobs are not insignificant, nor indeed are they unimportant to the local economy, but local opposition is being ignored as it so often is in Scotland.

This wee illustration shows the difference between a small country with economic and financial power able to respond to local needs and requirements, and prepared to do so, and a large Government, with many interests to attend to, which has no knowledge of, or interest in, small communities which have little political power.

Lessons to be drawn.

One of the most powerful lessons I draw from international comparisons is that control of its domestic currency is vital for any independent Government. If it has not got control of its currency, is it really independent in the present world? Is Greece an independent country, when decisions made by its people and its parliament can be rejected by the banks?

We have looked at only a few countries so we can't be certain that this comparison holds on a wider basis, but if you look around the world, on a more extensive and wider study, I think you will find, as I have, that control of domestic currency, monetary policy and supply, coupled with a clear Government economic development policy is central to effective economic development. Look at Singapore, Look at Hong Kong.

The neo-liberal philosophy which now dominates in Western society has become the foundation of a new international elite which is embedded in the financial system like a parasite which has buried into the central organs of its host and can't be dislodged without killing the host.

It is not a new phenomenon, indeed in the early years of the twentieth century this idea of the financial leadership being organised on an international basis, was discussed at the US Banking Association in 1924* by Montagu Norman, then Governor of the Bank of England. He told them "Capital must protect itself in every possible way." One of the ways he suggested was to "make the common people more docile, and governed by a strong arm with central power under leading financiers"

Two significant things we know about Montagu Norman, one is that he was a financial supporter of Adolf Hitler and the Nazi party in its establishment, so that gives us some notion of what his idea was of a 'docile common people governed by a strong arm'. His efforts in this regard were dramatically unsuccessful, but only at the cost of massive death destruction and untold suffering for the common people.

However the second thing we know about him was related to his banking organisational skills and in this he was more successful, indeed his main project, which is still flourishing today; was his efforts to establish the BIS, the 'Bank of International Settlement' in Switzerland. The BIS is an international banker's bank which has an interesting role in international financial affairs. Baring in mind Norman's objective that "capital must protect itself" it is reasonable for us to assume that the BIS has that as its main objective.

Now all this happened before the Great Wall Street crash in 1929 and before Hitler came to power in 1933 so does it have any relevance today in the 21st century? Well, yes there is still a link today, through the BIS established my Montagu Norman, which is still at the centre of the Western World's financial system.

Professor Carroll Quigley, is not a well know academic, he is a professor at Georgetown University and is sometimes described as mentor of Ex-Us President Bill Clinton. In his book 'Tragedy and Hope'* he makes reference to the secret world of international finance. He claims that while the IMF is the public face of international finance; the 'real' shadow face is the BIS which is the top central bank to 60 national central banks handling a staggering 95% of the Western World's money, with no transparency or accountability. He claims that "The substantial financial powers of the world are in the hands of these investment bankers who remain largely behind the scenes" He also tells us that the international leadership continue to meet every two months to plan international financial strategy.

So what is all this background structure for? After all, we know from economics that money has no intrinsic value, particularly today when all the currencies are fiat currencies (just paper money) and are not supported by gold.

It is interesting that when Montagu Norman was very concerned about 'protecting capital' he was the Governor of the BoE in 1924, and that the gold standard was abandoned in England in 1925. Montagu Norman would have been well aware of the pressure to abolish the gold standard leaving the pound with only the fig leaf of 'confidence' to cover its nakedness.

This protection of financial capital, it would appear, was therefore the long term protection of fiat currencies and their power to make phantom money from the fractional-reserve banking system. If this was their objective they required to get political protection for this corrupt system and to maintain this. This might explain their need for regular meetings at international level to ensure the political insurance cover is being maintained.

Domestic Currency

With this level of corruption and central control of Western fiat currencies at international level it does not require much imagination to see that any small politically independent state in the geographical region of its influence, can't escape the tentacles of this monster.

However it is equally clear that some are much more at its mercy than others.

The main thing to avoid is that you allow the private banking system to have control of your domestic currency, because this affects the greatest part of the country's economy and the direct link for the Government between public investment and economic development. If you lose that link, then you lose control of your economy, although of course you still have responsibility for the debts which the banking system will create for you.

So the objectives of any independent state which wants to retain its economic independence is

(1)   Take, and maintain, control of your domestic currency.

(2)   Convert your domestic currency to a full-reserve currency and

(3)   don't allow your foreign exchange currency to corrupt your domestic currency

If you can't manage all three of these, try to manage the first two. Because if you do manage the first two you will have a national base within which you can fight to control your national currency and your economy and this is the most important matter for the people.

Before concluding this chapter I will by go over once again the con-trick at the heart of the fractional-reserve banking system.

If I was to discover a printing machine which could make a perfect copy of a BoE £20 note and I installed that in my garden shed and used it to print £400 worth of bank notes every week and put them into general circulation that would be a criminal offense.

Now suppose I worked at a bank and earned £400 each week for my legitimate work, and that in addition to my wages I printed another £400 and I put that £400 of counterfeit notes into the bank safe each week and took out £400 in valid notes in exchange, in order to get my counterfeit notes into circulation without difficulty. That would also be a criminal offence and 50% of my earnings would be the proceeds of crime.

However, if I decided to open up my own bank, and used the £400 per week I was making from my counterfeiting activity to lend to others charging them interest on that money. If I did that I would be doing practically the same thing as a fractional-reserve bank is doing every day, yet such activity would be legal for a bank in the UK, USA and Europe.

Now of course I would not be allowed to do that, because I would need support from the Banking Association to set up a bank, and that would not be possible on such a small scale.

If I was well connected, went to the right school and was on the team as it were, then with such support I could possible do it legally, but only on a much greater scale. What is illegal for me as an ordinary citizen to do on a small scale becomes entirely legal, even laudable, for me to do if I have the right connection in the financial sector, but only if I were to do this on a grand scale. Where is the economic or legal validity in that?

Now some might see this as a victimless crime. This appears to be a crime which does not injury anyone.

However in earlier times society was well aware of this crime, it was considered one of the greatest crimes one could commit and was punished by the death penalty in most cases.

Because, of course, this is not a victimless crime; on the contrary this is a crime which defaces and devalues the money for everyone else. This would no doubt go unnoticed in the small example I gave, but in the real world today with massive amounts of phantom money being created and circulated by the banking system in every fiat currency in all Western countries the scale of the problem is gigantic and is now completely out of control. Like any parasite which feeds on the vital organs of its host, it eventually prevents the host from functioning properly, and in this case it strangles the real economy.

It is not accidental that finding 'money' for sound economic development of industry is very difficult, while savings is not rewarded and the financial system is awash with cheap money for speculation and quick turnover.

So when the Scottish people get the next opportunity to vote for political independence they will be increasingly conscious of the growing economic problems within the UK, Europe and the US and will be looking for answers to the problems which these great powers can't handle. We must be able to show them that a vote for Scottish independence opens the door to economic independence, the end of austerity and towards economic growth and development. If we are confident and can identify the way forward which rejects 'austerity' then people will be interested and we will win their confidence and support.

Scotland's currency.

Historically Scotland is in a very good position to escape from the fractional-reserve banking parasite. Scots were among the first people in the world to study and experiment with banking ideas and this gave them great experience which they learned to apply over time so a short history of Scottish banking experience is worth considering.

After the death of Queen Elizabeth the 1st of England James the 6th of Scotland took the English Throne in addition to his Scottish Throne and became James the 1st of England in 1603 and moved to London. James took a number of people with him when his 'Scottish Court' moved to London. George Heriot was the Queen's, Edinburgh Jeweller at the time. George went to London with them. Heriot was a goldsmith and set up business in London. In those days goldsmiths acted as the early bankers.

Heriot later became King James' banker and also close associate. He is renowned for his wealth and because he was always handling jewellery he was called 'Jinglin Geordie' in Edinburgh. He became well known for his charitable work and his name lives on in Edinburgh in many street names, in Heriot-Watt University and in an interesting wee pub in one of the lanes off the Royal Mile.

George Heriot soon built up a powerful goldsmith business in London and was one of the early bankers in both London and Edinburgh. He was among the first of the Scots to earn the name of the 'canny Scot' operating in the financial world. There were of course a great number of Scots in the King's Scots Court who were living in London so this was the original basis for George Heriot's goldsmith/banking business.

By the late 17th century Scots involved in the goldsmith and early banking business were common in London and Scotland. It was therefore no surprise that William Paterson from the Scottish Border Country was, in 1691 discussing establishing a scheme to put together a £1.2 million loan for King William 111 on the basis of an 8% per annum interest return. This proposal, based on loans raised by Paterson, became the basis of the new Bank of England which was established in 1694 to service this arranged loan.

The same William Paterson then established the Bank of Scotland in 1695. He then raised £500,000 for the Darien Scheme, for a Scottish colony in Panama from investors mainly in Scotland. This scheme of his failed spectacularly. Paterson and the Scots, many of whom had invested heavily in the Darien Scheme, got a powerful lesson from the failure of this scheme and the huge cost to Scotland. They had learned a great deal from their success in banking, but they learned even more from their failure in early banking adventures.

In the early 19th century Scotland paid attention to the development of banking in the Netherlands who were developing banking on a Joint-stock company basis and adopted that approach. England on the other hand did not. In 1825 there was a major crisis in UK banking which spread from England right across the British Empire, Europe and South America. John Turner in his book 'Banking in Crisis' * claims "There have been two major or systemic banking crises in the past two centuries 1825-6 and 2007-8" So he sees the 1825 crisis in the English banking system as a systemic failure of great significance.

In England the banking system developed fairly slowly initially. By 1750 for example there were only 12 banks in England outside London. However after that there was an explosion in bank growth by 1810 there were 800 banks outside London, however these banks were not well founded or stable and were failing on an increasing rate from 1815. In the crisis in 1825, 61 English banks collapsed. George Robb* says about that "Critics delighted in contrasting the English banks with their Scottish counterparts, which had long been organised along joint-stock principles and which weathered the 1825 crisis without a hitch"

So Scotland had a reputation for prudent banking and the English banking system following the 1825 crash copied Scotland's example in this field.

Scotland retained a reputation for sound banking practice and experience for many years, indeed many currencies like the Singapore, and Hong Kong dollars were originally set-up by Scottish bankers, this reputation held right up until the end of the 20th century. Thatcher's 'reforms' however undermined the regulations which underpinned the Scottish banking approach and rendered Scottish Bank qualifications unhelpful and surplus to requirements.

As a result many of those who were in charge of 'Scottish' banks in the 2007 crisis did not hold Scottish Banking Qualifications, which by that time were considered irrelevant.

The Scottish pound

Unlike any other example I am aware of, the current situation in Scotland provides Scotland's Government with no control over currency, or monetary policy, or money supply; but does allow certain 'Scottish' banks to produce 'Scottish' bank notes which are on a par with the pound sterling. These 'Scottish' pound notes are, in effect, a full-reserve currency. Because any bank which issues such notes, must supply a pound sterling to the Bank of England reserves for every 'Scottish' pound it issues. So for each Scottish note in circulation there is a pound sterling in reserve in the BoE. Now that constitutes a full-reserve system within the sterling system.

Now it seems to me, keeping in mind that currency changes should not take place on the surface if they can be more effectively carried out away from public sight, that we have a great opportunity to do that in Scotland with the Scottish pound.

Instead of these notes being printed by certain private banks, we make the new Scottish National Bank the only authorised bank to issue currency. Instead of them depositing a pound on pound reserve in the BoE they deposit this reserve in the SNB. The Scottish Government then legislates to ensure that the SNB has control of money supply and is responsible for monetary policy implication. Then, with virtually nothing changing on the surface, we will have converted the Scottish pound into a full reserve currency under Scottish Government control.

Major changes could be brought about with virtually nothing appearing to have changed above the surface of the financial iceberg.

In effect therefore Scotland already has a full-reserve currency, only it is one that is not controlled by the Government but by private banks.

So in stark contrast with some of the countries we have been making comparisons with Scotland has the existing appearance of its own domestic currency which is currently full-reserve. This image could be made into reality, after political independence, by a few significant changes in the submerged part of the financial iceberg.

So with its long experience in banking, Scotland should be in a very good position when it decided to have political independence to establish a full-reserve currency controlled by the Government which can effectively address Scotland's economic requirements. It will be able to do this with very little change in the current financial system we Scots are familiar with so there should, on the surface be no reason for concern.

Yet by making significant changes to the financial iceberg below the surface, we could protect the Scottish currency and the Scottish economy in a time then there is an international problem in the Western World.

* You-Tube www.youtube.com/watch?v=e2VuElk5_Bg

* United Nations economic commission for Latin America and the Caribbean.

* Speech of Montagu Norman, Gov; Bank of England to US Banking Association 1924 NY

* Carroll Quigley 'Tragedy and Hope' Georgetown University

* John D Turner 'Banking in Crisis' Cambridge University Press

* George Robb 'White-Collar Crime in Modern England' Cambridge University Press

Chapter 6

Scottish Sovereignty

In any consideration of Scottish Independence the question of sovereignty arises, but often in a somewhat confused fashion. For example we get some people who will tell you that they want Scottish independence with the present Queen as sovereign.

Now in any descriptive sense it would be impossible for Scotland to be 'independent' if anyone was to be considered 'sovereign'. This idea is just a contradiction in terms. What is presumably meant by this is a politically independent democratic Scotland, with a none-political figurehead as the nominal 'Head of State'.

I believe that in important issues such as this there should be no room for ambiguity. Indeed ambiguity in this area is dangerous for the stability of the state. It is therefore of importance that everyone is quite clear about the question of sovereignty in Scotland today and in the future. So what is Scottish Sovereignty, and how is it defined?

That question is a bit like, what is Scotland as an entity? What is the essence of Scotland?

This particular question was starkly faced by all the people living in Scotland at the end of the 13th and the beginning of the 14th centuries during Scotland's bitter struggle for survival in the wars of independence against England. Beginning with King John Balliol, then Wallace, then Robert Bruce, all these in turn, led the Scots, in this struggle to establish Scottish Independence and Scottish Sovereignty. Fortunately near the end of that struggle, only six years after the decisive battle of Bannockburn, the Scottish parliament put this idea firmly in writing which we can all now read.

This written form of the concept of Scottish sovereignty was put together in a letter written to the Pope in 1320 which we know today as the 'Declaration of Arbroath'. This document was constructed and supported by people who knew what the cost of fighting for independence really was. We think we have suffered because we were been deceived and cheated and beaten in a referendum. They suffered much more than we can imagine. They lost friends and family and endured the most severe hardship for many years in the fight for independence. So their definition of Scottish Sovereignty is worthy of our attention and indeed respect.

They saw the King, as head of state, as being in a very significant position in Scottish sovereignty, as of course we would expect in a feudal society in which the king played a central role; but they did not identify the King as ultimate sovereign. Indeed they specifically wrote that King Robert the Bruce was the legitimate King of Scots, but that if he failed to defend the people's independent rights they would remove him, and replace him with another who would. That is the essence of the Declaration of Arbroath. The King, Robert the Bruce, was the true king and ruler of Scotland, but the sovereign power remained with the people. Ultimate sovereign power lay in the hands of the people, not the King.

I believe this definition of sovereignty is unique to Scotland in feudal Europe, I do not believe you will find another, so publicly declared, claim of the sovereignty of the people anywhere else in Feudal Europe. I doubt also if you will find a people in Europe who fought so tirelessly for their independence as the Scots did. It is therefore a hard won principle of our cultural inheritance and one which we should cherish and certainly not lose by neglect.

Some will tell you that that particular concept of sovereignty was sold out by the Scottish Parliament in 1707 by a 'parcel of rogues' in the Treaty of Union. Well, it was not; indeed it was not even addressed in the Treaty of Union. The Treaty was concerned with the creation of a new British Parliament, which was in effect just an extension of the Westminster Parliament. The English Parliament was not concerned with sovereignty in this regard, their view of sovereignty was quite distinct from the Scottish view and they believed they had this in hand.

The English Parliament had passed the Act of Settlement in 1701 which they considered had settled the question of the royal succession and for them this addressed the sovereignty issue.

The English had, of course, an entirely different concept of sovereignty. Their view of sovereignty was contained in the concept of 'the king in parliament' which had come from the struggle between the English King John and his Barons resulting in the Magna Carta Treaty in 1215, which was soon broken, but which later in Edward the 1st time developed into the idea that sovereignty resided in the 'King in parliament'. This concept does not, give any credence to 'the people' they do not figure in it at all, it is just the institutions 'King' and 'Parliament' that are important.

When we appreciate that in the 13th century England the King, and indeed the parliament in England were composed of Normans who had imposed themselves on the native Saxon people and ruled over them, not with them, then you can see the big distinction between the two concepts. The Norman rulers in 13th century England spoke a different language from the ordinary people and had very little in common with them.

Bruce and many of his leading supporters were also of Norman decent, but Bruce had been rejected by the Norman hierarchy and was forced to depend on the common people of Scotland who were a mixture of Gaelic speaking Highland Scots, Scots speaking Lowland Scots, Normans, English, Norse and Flemings. Like Scotland today the Scots in 1320 were a mixed bunch. However this mixed bunch of people with their different cultures and languages united to support Bruce and they were then considered central to Scotland's independence. This mixed bunch of common people won Scotland's independence by their efforts, and maintained it for centuries against constant attack from their larger neighbour.

Therefore at the time of the Treaty of Union the English negotiators were not concerned with sovereignty as an idea, they believed that they had dealt with that in the Act of Settlement in 1701, which would be fully effective once the new parliament, which they would control, was established. So they were not unduly concerned about sovereignty, and the Scots never addressed it.

Therefore the ancient Scottish concept of sovereignty, put in writing by the Scottish parliament in 1320, accepted by the Scottish King and by the pope, was well established as the definition of Scottish sovereignty and has never been challenged.

All legal processes depend on the idea of sovereignty. Any law, to be considered legitimate, must have the stamp of sovereign approval. To-day this is covered in Statute law by the 'Crown' consenting to a Parliamentary Act. In Common Law long unchallenged precedent, acts as confirmation of 'Crown' approval. Now the Scottish concept of sovereignty has both; it was passed by a Scottish parliament, approved by the king and has remained unchallenged in Scotland for nearly 700 years.

The fact that the current Scotland Act going through the Westminster parliament did not contain a clause allowing the Scottish people to organise a referendum for Scottish independence is in fact irrelevant.

The Scottish Government, with the approval of the majority of the Scottish people has full sovereign authority to do this, it does not require any authority from the Westminster Parliament, and indeed the Westminster Parliament does not hold Scottish sovereignty, so it can't grant it in any event.

Scotland would indeed have backing from the United Nations for the right to determine its own political future under the UN Charter article 1.2 according to Craig Murray ex-UK Ambassador. So our ancient heritage on the question of sovereignty has now become the accepted view in international relations, and international law. It is the old fashioned English 'king in Parliament' definition which is now out-of-date in the modern world.

The suggestion that we can only have a 'legal' right to organise a referendum in Scotland, if Westminster grants it, has no sound basis in Scottish or international law. Because all law requires to be the will of the sovereign in order to be legitimate. If the 'sovereign' in Scotland is the people, then what they explicitly decide, or is decided on their behalf by an elected Government, which they do not object to, is Lawful.

We therefore need waste no time on any concern about this issue. The situation in Spain is of interest. Can the people in Catalonia decide to leave Spain, if the Spanish courts claim that this is illegal? Well, we may well see how this plays out on the international stage.

Compared with Scottish sovereignty the Spanish/Catalan issue does not have anything like the historical background. In this case the modern view as expressed in the UN Charter is probably much more appropriate

Land and Territorial rights.

Sovereignty and nationality also embodies the idea of a distinct land, an identifiable area of land which defines the borders of the country. Indeed it is normally the land, rather than the distinct people, that identifies the nation. So a nation and the distinct land that the nation holds are important in the concept of nationality.

The modern Scots view of nationality has nothing to do with race or ethnic origin of the people. It simply relates to where people live. So a Scot in the new Scotland may have been born in Cape Town, or Dublin or Berlin or Newcastle, and can be black, white or mixed colour and have any, or no religion; it is where he or she currently resides that determines their Scottish citizenship. That indeed was how it was defined in the independence referendum and that view seems to have been widely accepted in Scotland

Now land ownership and Scotland's territorial waters have been much abused over the years. However when the Scottish people decide to establish political independence they will at the same time confirm Scottish Government control over all Scottish land and territorial waters. These boundaries would be established by international law, not as currently established by UK 'administrative' allocation. This in itself will return a huge area of territorial waters, which are currently claimed to be English under UK 'administrative' arrangements.

Scottish land borders would no doubt be based on the borders that existed in 1707 while territorial waters would be defined by the current international treaties which apply in relation to that land and the islands it contains. This would result in a clear, internationally agree, land, sea and air space which was identified as Scottish.

Now if Scottish sovereignty is in the hands of the people, and if the Scottish people have a duty to defend and protect their land, it follows that the Scottish people must have the final say over all Scottish land

In 1320 when the Scot's were writing to define their sovereignty, land was not referred to, other than to identify Scotland. Land at that time in the feudal system was considered to be in the hands of the King to grant, on feudal terms, to the aristocracy. He could grant land, and take it away. The king had control over the land, but as we have seen in Scottish sovereignty the power to remove the king, rested with the people. So ultimately the people had final say over the land in feudal Scotland.

So in the new Scotland we must ensure that the people have the final say on sovereignty and on all land, territorial waters, air space and natural resources.

Now, it is not difficult to see the link between sovereignty and the land, and it seems reasonable, and only fair that if I have rights and responsibilities as a citizen of Scotland towards the sovereignty and the land, then I must also share in the ultimate decision making as to the use of that land.

When I was just 18 years old I was in Aden with a loaded rifle defending 'British' territory, and some of the young men with me were conscripts. That is they were forced to become a soldier and to defend British territory with their lives, even if that territory was a very long way from Briton.

If your country gives you rights as a citizen and responsibilities, such as putting your life on the line to defend land, then it seems to me that the 'land' you are defending should be the land where you have the citizenship and you should have a joint right to have a say about the use of that land if you have a joint responsibility to defend it.

I entirely accept the principle that 'with rights comes responsibilities' Every child born in Scotland, irrespective of ethical or cultural background will be given free Scottish citizenship and all rights connected with that. Free health care, free education, etc; however they will also be expected to accept responsibility when old enough, to work to pay for these services, to defend the country and its people, to fully participate in the democratic process, etc.

Now the best way to ensure that all citizens get their entitlement to fair human rights is to set this down in a written constitution. Something the UK has not got. It is however something which the new Scotland must have, and few would dispute that the sovereignty of the people and their rights and obligation in relation the land. Also of course, people's legal and human rights need to be established in a written constitution if they are to be protected over time. So there are good grounds for having a written constitution and I will return to this idea later.

Defending Land

Most of us can see without difficulty why we should be prepared to fight to defend our freedom and democracy so I will not address that, but what about land? Did it make sense for young Scots men and women to be obliged to fight and die to help the UK to hold onto the Falkland Islands?

We had obligations to the people on these islands we are told. Well that I can accept, this is an obligation which we who live in the UK did have, but it is an obligation we could have met quite easily by providing land and resettlement support for every family in the Falkland Islands to come to the UK.

Scotland alone could have provided land more appropriate than the windswept freezing South Atlantic for this rural people. We could have helped them, and they could have helped us at a tiny fraction of the cost of the Falklands war, and no mother would have wept for a lost son or daughter.

If young Scots in future are to put their lives on the line to defend 'land' we should make it clear just 'what land' they will be asked to defend. If we spell out clearly in our constitution that Scotland has no territorial ambitions and will not use military force outwith our own territory, other than to support the United Nations, or to help defend a neighbour, at that neighbour's specific request. Then the Scottish people and others abroad will know where we stand on this.

If people in the Falkland Islands, or Gibraltar, or any other small piece of land elsewhere in the world want our help, we should not fail to respond to them, but fighting to hold land in some place far from Scotland should not be permitted under the Scottish Constitution and we must make it clear that we will not do that.

As for the land and territorial waters in Scotland all of these must come under Scottish Government control and remain so. Now again we will be told that much of this land is privately owned, and a lot of it is owned by people, or companies which can't be identified. So we have no authority over that land.

The French philosopher Jean-Jacques Rousseau wrote "He who first put a fense around a piece of land and found people prepared to accept that he owned it, was the true founder of civil society"* What Rousseau was saying is that anyone who could convince others that the land belonged to him as a personal possession was the greatest of all confidence fraudster if he found people stupid enough to believe him. It is as absurd as the suggestion that I own the air in my garden. People of course have the exclusive rights to work land, but ownership is quite different.

If, like Rousseau we find the claim of personal ownership of land illogical and without foundation, then we must recognise that the Scottish people have the sovereign power over all Scotland's land. Any who lay claims to this land need to do so within the terms set by the people or their elected Government on their behalf. The idea that any individual owns a part of Scotland and has absolute rights to it, irrespective of the effects of that on others is illogical, impractical and unacceptable.

Our Constitution must make it clear that the land in Scotland and its territorial waters comes under the sovereignty of the Scottish people and always will remain so, whatever arrangements are currently being applied in its use.

All Scottish land needs to be registered, and as a precise natural resource a land tax should be applied to all land. Of course for land used for housing a zero-rate tax can be applied all the time it is being used for that purpose. This would apply to land used for agriculture and other productive activity. So that land used to the benefit of the Scottish people would be zero-rated so tax free. However land which was not used in this way would be taxed annually. So anyone holding land or changing land use, would be required to pay the land tax, unless he/she could show that this land use was awarded a zero-rate clearance.

This would mean that all current holders of land would need to acknowledge their, or their company's, claim on the land. If the tax was not paid, or if no claim was made in respect of any land the state should take possession of such land, which could in turn be allocated to those who had an approved use for it.

Such an approach would deal with the 'problem' of hidden landowners and people holding hand purely to take advantage of rising land prices resulting from shortage of available land. It would also address the scandal of working farmers being forced off the land at the behest of some landowner who thinks he/she can take advantage of their 'ownership' to make a more profitable deal.

I take the view that land, and its use and control is part of Scottish sovereignty and must be part of our written constitution. Our young people may in the future, have to fight and die for our land, as they have often done in the past. In future however, in an independent Scotland they will know, not only about their obligations to defend our land, but also about their rights in relation to Scottish land, which must be set out in our constitution.

Constitutional Currency.

In the book 'Moving On' we raised the issue of 'constitutional money' in which we placed the Scottish currency in the important position of having full-reserve status, its supply and its regulation, specifically covered in the written constitution. It seems to me that there is a very sound case for this in the new independent Scotland which we want to build. It may be, as people start to see the old certainties of the Western currencies crumble and fail that people will be looking more carefully at this in the future.

I have made it obvious already in this book that I expect to see problems in the Western financial system before long and this will bring even more hardship and suffering to people than it is doing currently. If I am right about that, then people will be more careful and more concerned about paper currency than they have been in the recent past.

This subject is almost banned from open discussion, it is considered to be in very poor taste for anyone to talk publicly about the inevitability of the pound failing. After all, we are reminded, the pound relies on public confidence, and so people like me who question its sustainability are encouraging others to lose faith in the pound and undermining confidence in it. This is in some people's eyes tantamount to being a traitor to the country.

Those of us who wish to address and deal with this problem must ignore this and must be frank about the difficulties and not only address them, but address problems which could arise with such currencies in the future and how best to guard against them.

If we take sensible steps to safeguard out national currency, then we will need to be prepared to keep a constant guard on this. It is said that the price of democratic freedom is constant vigilance; which is undoubtedly true. It can also be said that the same is true for a safe and secure currency. The most effective way to ensure this vigilance is maintained in the long-term is to set-down the main arrangements for the currency in the constitution in such a way that it can't be easily put aside by a future Government to meet some temporary 'emergency' and then lost forever.

The idea of asking people to put their trust in a 'piece of paper' based on a promise from a Government that this 'piece of paper' will secure this Government's promise over time and across national borders and in all circumstances; is difficult enough. If people have just witnessed some spectacular failures in such systems, it will become even more difficult.

Therefore if a new independent Scotland wants to convince people that they should have confidence in Scotland's new currency we will need to show them that we have learned the lessons of recent financial history and are taking effective steps to protect our currency. So we should display the fact that we placed it in a position where it can't be corrupted by speculators.

A citizen of the new Scotland must be reassured not only that his/her democratic and human rights are safe, but that the Scottish land and currency will remain firmly in Scottish Government control and won't be sold off to private speculators who can use them for personal gain and against the vital interests of the Scottish people.

Written Constitution.

Of course constructing a suitable written constitution for the new Scotland, must be done democratically and openly. The Icelandic idea of mass involvement in the debate about the constitution is an attractive idea. What is clear is that if we are going to do this properly it will take time. Getting it right will be much more important than getting it quick. So although we may have plenty of ideas about the constitution the document itself will not be put together until well after we have established independence.

Our new Constitution needs to carry over the valuable parts of our cultural heritage from the past, like the concept of sovereignty resting ultimately with the people, although of course, the wording of the written Constitution would up-date the written statement set-down in the Declaration of Arbroath, but it would take forward the same idea.

A written constitution is a vital part of the Governing structure of a modern state because it spells out the rights and obligation which rest on the citizens and the institutions in society and this clarity alone enhances the freedom of the individual. If however this constitution is to have maximum value for the citizen it must address the fundamental issues relating to his/her life, health, prosperity and relationships.

A constitution of pious ambiguous sentiments is of no value to anyone, we all agree that "the pursuit of happiness" sounds like a great idea but we don't quite know what it means. Our constitution must give us clear ideas such as the idea that "ultimate sovereignty rests with the people" and spell out how this applies today. This means that any system, no matter how old or renowned, must be rejected if the people make a clear majority decision to do that.

In this context it is obvious that where the National State has obligation to the citizens, such as responsibility for the national territory, or the national currency, then this responsibility should be spelt out, and how this responsibility will be maintained. Because this type of written commitment would then be significant in the legal process and could be used by individuals to assert their rights.

Since the written constitution carries forward the fundamental 'contract' between the people and any particular elected Government it must be strong enough to prevent any elected Government from putting it to one side; while at the same time flexible enough to be taken to the people to allow amendments and additions which are felt to be required by the elected Government, or by common demand.

The very loose arrangement in the UK which has no written constitution as such will not be adequate for the new modern Scotland, because it gives the establishment and those with political power the ability to interpret the constitution in the way they prefer to.

Now many will say they want a written constitution, and much I have said here they will not disagree with. They may however find it strange that I should include 'land' in the constitution. I think you will see from what I have written above that territory is important and that land should have a place in the Constitution. The area that many will find quite new and radical is to include currency in the Constitution.

I make no apology for insisting that this important issue is addressed and placed at the highest level in our new democratic Scotland. Indeed the failure to give this issue the attention and consideration it requires has led to us loosing the referendum, so it is time we started to give this matter more attention.

My view is that currency is at the very centre of the parasite which is destroying the Western world economies. If I am right then it makes sense to take effective action to protect the Scottish people from this parasite, and to prevent it from getting into the lives-blood of the New Scotland. If we want a modern constitution which will endure it must be able to govern a modern complex society and any society with a fiat currency must have strict control and regulation of the currency or the currency and the economy will be ruined.

The Government can establish a new full-reserve Scottish pound and can reform the banking system to control monetary policy and money supply, but in order to provide long-term security of its financial system it will need to have it firmly based on principles enshrined in the constitution.

Government's first duty it is said is to protect the people, but surely its second duty is to protect their livelihood and their national assets. The threat to a modern country comes in many ways. Perhaps an undermining of the economy by corrupting the currency is high on the list of dangers which the new independent Scotland will be faced with.

The way forward.

The Scottish Government talks about valid reasons for a second referendum, while doing so the First Minister has made it clear on a number of occasions that any decision on that rested with the Scottish people. In this she is absolutely right, the Scottish people, and the Scottish people alone, will make this decision.

We can of course speculate on what might trigger the Scottish people to want to reopen this and organise another referendum, but this is only pure speculation and means nothing unless the Scottish people start moving towards a significant change.

Well, how will we know when this is happening? Does it not need Government guidance?

The answer to the first question is that the Scottish people are on the move right now, the major change in people's opinion which is reflected in the dramatic change in voting patterns, never before witnessed on this scale in Scottish democratic history, tells us that public opinion is changing. The 'official' privately owned media like to claim that they know and can tell us about public opinion, but they can't; none of them could see this change until it happened. Even now most of the media have not accepted, or adjusted to this change.

However social media is much better at picking up this change in public mood. This movement in public opinion once started is likely to continue for some time before it settles down and it is reasonable to consider that the motivating force behind it will determine its strength and direction.

So what is this motivating force?

It appears to me that people are becoming increasingly aware that the society they live in is changing and becoming more unsafe and insecure for them and their families. When they look to the politicians they have traditionally looked to for reassurance or support, they are finding that the politicians are refusing to address their concerns, or pretending that they are not there. People are increasingly feeling 'alienated' in their own environment. Jimmy Reid in his Rectorial address to Glasgow University in 1972 addressed this issue specifically, Jimmy, as usual was spot-on in his observations on this. I will return to this and give it more consideration in the final chapter, but at this stage I want to identify it with the major political movement we are seeing in Scotland.

This alienation I believe goes some way to explain why people in large numbers have started to change. Now to address the question of Government guidance to people, in this regard I do not think that this is happening, or can happen to any great extent. If as I believe, the main motivation force is driven by alienation of the people, then it has a long development period and did not happen as a result of recent event. Recent events, and indeed current events, might provoke the people and increase the movement for change, but they did not start it in the first place.

It is vital for the SNP Government, and for all of us in the independence movement to recognise that the Scottish people are on the move, and it would be foolish for any of us to believe that our political activity has created this movement, or can easily direct it.

There is no doubt that the SNP call for an independence referendum, and the campaign to secure a Yes vote, triggered something among the

Scottish people and created a catalyst as it were, to a potential movement for change. This movement was not just about Scottish independence. Scottish independence was just one option for the change this movement was seeking. That is why, contrary to all experience and expectation this movement did not stop when the referendum was over, but continued to move and is still moving.

So where is this movement taking us?

Before I rush in with an easy answer to that, I have to confess that I do not know the answer. It may be that even people caught up in the force of the movement do not know the answer themselves. If indeed the motivation power is driven by alienation the answer would seem to be the need for people to feel that they, as individuals, do have a role in this society and can play a positive moral role. This they may see in an independent Scotland, but the general idea of an independent Scotland does not, by itself, assure this. Our task perhaps it to try to make sure it does.

If people in very significant numbers have started to look for a way to escape from the alienation and insecurity which they and their families are facing then, we as a movement must address this. We can do this, not just in some academic debate, but in the actions we take and practical proposals we make most particularly by involving the people in broader participation.

Why are we supporting Scottish Independence?

The reason why many people, myself included, are keen to see Scotland become an independent country, is not so that we can change the national flag and leave everything else untouched. Indeed the reason why political independence is so important to many of us is precisely because it gives us the opportunity to make big changes, big improvements.

The biggest single change we need is to increase significantly public investment into the Scottish economy, in order to create jobs and opportunities, particularly for our young people. Discussion on how to do this must be more progressive than the repeated nonsense we hear from traditional politicians. We need some practical and well designed plans which people can see and appreciate.

What is without doubt is that we can demonstrate that this can be done by highlighting examples and explaining how it can be work. One simple example is to examine what Jim McColl did in Greenock and explain the lessons to be taken from this. Not only for private investment but for public investment. When we show that Scotland's economy can be expanded in this way and that we will need an expanding external market to take up our substantial productive potential, we will capture people's attention. People will start to see hope and potential instead of fear and despair.

This approach we should also apply to other industrial situations in Scotland right now like the aluminium industry, and the steel industry, not only to help the families currently involved but also to show our wider vision for a more positive productive Scotland.

That is a bit of what was engendered in the independence campaign. We need to proceed along that road, but of course not with empty promises, but with real assessments of genuine potential. The new powers offered to Scotland in the infamous 'Vow' could, where they have any substance, and frankly most don't, be used to invest and develop our economy along Keynesian lines. However if we start to do that in the economic field we will quickly run into the money/currency bottleneck which exists in our colonial Scotland.

Now this is exactly why this book was written, because we must advance beyond this bottleneck and we can't do that without having a clear policy and understanding on the currency issue. While we are trapped in the sterling zone we will not be able to break this bottleneck, but it should become more obvious. The problem itself is not difficult, what appears to be difficult is getting people to face up to it, instead of looking the other way and pretending it does not exist.

Well, confronting this problem is the main reason why I am a supporter of Scottish independence; because without breaking from the UK and sterling and the present fractional-reserve banking system; this bottleneck can't be cleared. However with an independent Scotland which controlled its own currency this bottleneck can be cleared and we can succeed in our objective and fulfil our hopes.

It is almost certainly very difficult, if not impossible, for our economic and financial reforms to be carried out on a UK basis. With the UK and the City of London at the heart of the sterling system, any attempt to reform it in the way we are suggesting would create a massive upheaval in the social order, so this part of the world will be among the last to implement such reforms.

Scotland, on the other hand, although heavily involved in the sterling system, could be open to reform without major upheaval. Scotland with political independence could move forward to economic independence if it "took the bull by the horns" and moved forward. This would allow the Scots to reject austerity and to finance its own investment in a drive to a wealthy small modern state. It is interesting that at a recent 'Business for Scotland' function there was considerable recognition that local small business, and Scottish based international companies; had quite different agendas and objectives from large multi-national corporations.

I feel that there are good grounds for a sensible agreement between the Scottish and UK Governments on a currency/debt relief basis before the next referendum campaign debate starts. I think that there are compelling reasons for both sides to enter these negotiation and I think this needs to be spelt out so that there is no mistake. However irrespective of the way we approach this issue, we need to show the Scottish people that there is a way ahead and a bright future for them and their families, and indeed that their participation is required to bring this about.

If we can do this, we will retain the support of the Scottish people in increasing numbers and the political movement of the Scottish people will continue to run with us. In such circumstances we will have no difficulty identifying a reason for another referendum at a time of the Scottish Government's choice, which will meet with approval from the Scottish people. When we do this, and make sure that this time the ballot is properly conducted with a limited and controlled postal ballot, then the outcome of the referendum will be entirely predictable.

* Jean-Jacques Rousseau 'The social contract' 1762

* Rectorial address James Reid Bute Hall 28th April 1972

Chapter 7

Value of Money –Revision

In the introduction to this book I spent some time underlining the point that money, particularly in a fiat currency like the pound sterling, has no intrinsic value. I described this as a vital point and so indeed it is. What I want to do in this last reference to economics in the book is to demonstrate to you just how important this point is to an understanding of economics.

Recently I heard an 'expert' discussing the UK economy on the TV and he made the following point: "The IMF had been wrong to challenge George Osborne's policy on austerity because the UK had shown by a growth in GDP that the economy is growing again". Well that is an interesting statement, but is it necessarily true?

It would seem to be significant, because the Gross Domestic Product, GDP, is a collection of all goods and services produced in the country over the period of a year. We know that goods and services are real wealth, so it would seem that if the GDP has grown then real wealth must have increased.

However, this statement, pronounced with such certainty by a TV economics 'expert' is not necessarily true, indeed it in unlikely to be true. The main reason for this counter-intuitive assertion is because, here again, there is likely to be a situation in which we assume that money values are real values. We could indeed be taking 'money' values as the same thing as real value when we know that is not correct.

In this case one has to be very careful when discussing the measurement of the GDP as if it always actually reflected the accurate real measurement of goods and services. It is an attempt to do that of course, but it is a very crude and often an ineffective way of doing it.

How do you measure goods such as a ton of coal, a box of cod, and a new TV set together with a day's teaching, 6 haircuts and a heart operation? The only way this can be done is to convert them all into their equivalent in money at a given point in time. This gives you a cash figure which is equal to the sum of all these items of 'real' wealth at a specific point in time. This in effect is how the GDP is measured.

If you now contrast the money figure you get in any time period; with the figure you got the previous year by adding up all the costs of the goods and services, this could give you a good comparison, provided the proportions of the different ingredients did not change significantly, and relative prices remained stable. However if that does not happen you have problems making the adjustments.

In the real world these adjustment are very significant. In the last year oil prices fell sharply while land and house prices rose significantly, in some areas, yet not so significantly in others. All across the economy goods and services changed their relative prices, although their 'real' values remained pretty static. To illustrate this point the house I owned and lived in over the years changed its market value and its price on the market changed significantly mainly upwards, occasionally downwards, but its real value to me as a home did not change significantly in those years, whatever the market value was doing.

So real economic values, and money value are not the same thing; and the important value for understanding economics is 'real' values, not money inflated values. Now when you are considering figures in the region of 0 to 3% which need to be carefully adjusted to remove money changes you do not have a reliable way to measure growth in real wealth. This is particularly so when you see other figures showing employment rising while productivity is not improving, this tells a different story.

In normal circumstances in a manufacturing country moving from recession into growth productivity will improve as employment starts to rise. Now why is that? Well, the reason this happens is because productivity is closely related to new efficient technology. Now if a company is producing let's say, pots and pans, and is hit by recession it will start to reduce its output as demand falls, and naturally it will close the old and less efficient units first. When demand starts rising again it will not reopen old out of date systems, it will bring in new more efficient systems, and this will in most cases mean that productivity will rise.

Now if a manufacturing economy is starting to grow, after a long recession then you will see productivity rising as employment rises which means that as more people are employed even more goods and services are being produced for every new employee, so real wealth is growing. Now if that is not happening as in the UK at the moment, then you have to ask two questions (a) Why would a business employ more workers if it did not have the capital capacity to fully employ them? (b) Are these new jobs not real jobs with real wages which can contribute to real production and demand?

As you can see there are a number of factors, many of them more important than GDP figures, which tell us how the economy is performing. However if you really want to know how the UK economy has been doing in real terms over time, look at real living standards over a longer time span and make international comparisons on that. If you do that you will observe that the UK economy has been on the slide downwards for some considerable time. Nor does it look like changing any time soon.

Gordon Macintyre-Kemp, the CEO of Business for Scotland,* had an interesting article in the National newspaper on the 18th of December 2015 in which he wrote about the situation in the UK economy. "The economic system is broken" he writes, "not just taking a dip or struggling to recover, the fundamental flaw is now a crack that can't be papered over and major reform is needed now" Unfortunately for the UK such major reform is not likely, not now, nor in the foreseeable future, because too many powerful vested interests in the City will stop such reform. We in Scotland can, if we are wise, make our own arrangements for reform.

As you will see the view I am putting forward in this book about the UK economy is not very different from the position that Gordon takes in his article. What I hope is that in addition this book suggests a way out of this mess for the Scottish people provided we take the right steps to secure the right way out. It is not really sufficient to understand the problems the economy has, and to recognise that reform is urgent; it is necessary to show what reform is required and how to do it.

I hope this book helps with that.

Philosophy

In this final chapter of the book I want to look a bit wider than economics I want to consider philosophy. I don't want to quote Hume, Kant, Hobbes, Locke, Rousseau or any other renowned philosopher in some academic exercise. My objective is to do better than that and help to examine real philosophic ideas, in a real world setting, to see if it helps us to understand the current situation in Scotland.

The philosopher I have in mind is a Glasgow shipyard worker who was self-taught and well versed in his subject, and the work I have chosen to examine is Jimmy Reid's Rectorial address to Glasgow University in Bute Hall in the University on the 28th of April 1972.*

Jimmy's subject for that address was 'Alienation'. It was a short address, but packed full of understanding and insight. It has been considered by some as the most profound speech in the Western World since the Second World War, and it has been repeated and commented on right across the world. This is the famous 'The rat race is for rats' speech.

The very essence of what Jimmy put forward to the young students over 40 years ago, was that our society was creating a process of alienating people from the community in which they lived, in their working environment, in their political environment and even in their social environment. Jimmy describes this process as "It is the cry of men who feel themselves the victims of blind economic forces beyond their control. It's the frustration of ordinary people excluded from the processes of decision making. The feeling of despair and hopelessness that pervades people who feel with justification that they have no real say in shaping or determining their own destinies"

He explained that alienation was not new, but he believed then "it is more widespread, more pervasive than ever before". It was indeed, and since then it has grown somewhat. Jimmy put his finger on something which many would not have seen at that time. Indeed most of us tend not to see the wood for the trees. He however had singled out this phenomenon and focused on it.

He says that people may have dealt with this in different ways and at different levels, but he makes the vital point that whether or not people could articulate their feelings towards alienation, everyone could feel it. This of course is the most important aspect of this phenomenon, it is felt by everyone, no-one escapes it. It is in effect embodied in the general ideology within which our society operates.

Perhaps the most profound aspect of Jimmy's philosophy in this speech is to point out that everyone in a society which is geared towards alienating people, ends up losing out. Although there appears to be winners and losers in the rat race, in a real fundamental sense, there are not, we are all losers. To illustrate this point Jimmy quotes from the Bible "What doth it profit a man if he gain the whole world and suffer the loss of his own soul?"

The important part of this insight makes it clear that this is not something caused by wicked men or women who are deliberately creating this situation out of personal malice. It is much more serious than that; it is a process which damages everyone, those who assist its spread and those who are destroyed by it. We should not as, Jimmy points out, be angry with those who advance it, because they are also victims. Our best defence against this phenomenon is to understand what it is and to collectively deal with it at source.

Jimmy makes a telling point in his speech he says "The untapped resources of the North Sea are as nothing compared to the untapped resources of our people" In this statement again he was spot-on with his insight. The massive loss of production to Scotland caused by unemployment, under-employment, inadequate-employment and lost opportunity for our people is staggering in real economic terms.

If this can be put right, not only would it make Scotland a much happier, healthier and more secure place; but it would make it a very wealthy place both in a personal and in a community sense. Again Jimmy rightly identified the key to challenging this social phenomenon as education and enlightenment.

Well that is interesting, but what has it to do with the subject of this book, currency and economics?

I would suggest that it has a great deal to do with the problems in our present society, and the financial and economic issues they are confronted with. I would further suggest that it explains the major shift in political trust which has started to take place in Scotland which is of a magnitude never before seen in Scotland since the franchise was extended on a wide basis. The surge to the Labour party in the immediate post war period was significant but nothing like as dramatic as the 2015 General Election. If I am right in this regard then it is vital, for any political organisation, to study this and try to understand it.

Some people have described this political movement as like a shift in the tectonic plates.

I would partly agree with that, but not entirely.

A shift in the tectonic plates is movement which has its origins deep below the earth's crust and so, once it is on the move, there is nothing on the surface of the earth which can change that.

The belief that recent changes in political alignment are very deep rooted I do agree with. They are not the result of minor changes in any political party. They have deep profound cause in our social structure. So to that extent, I agree with the tectonic plates' comparison. I do not agree however, that we are unable to alter or significantly influence the cause of this phenomenon, I think we can. I do not suggest that this will be easy or that it can be done quickly, but I do believe that we can identify the cause and that we can effectively take steps to get in line with it and hopefully help to meet its aspirations.

Indeed I believe the cause of this major shift in political allegiance comes from the very phenomenon that Jimmy Reid was warning us about; the increasing alienation of people in our society. The causes which Jimmy identified as behind this increasing alienation have all got worse in the 40 years since his speech. Not of course in a regular progression, but in the longer term trend.

Jimmy delivered this speech near the end of the Upper Clyde Shipyards (UCS) campaign. At that time, there was considerable unrest in the labour movement in the UK. The miners had been on a National Strike in January and February 1972 which had ended with a miner's victory, but the gains of that victory were already being eroded by the time Jimmy was giving his address. The UCS campaign itself gave a great boost to working people in Scotland and elsewhere in the UK and by February 1974 the Miners were on a National Strike again to recover the ground they had lost. The Tory Heath Government called a snap General Election during the Miner's strike in an attempt to use the dispute to their political advantage, but lost out badly when they lost the election and Labour was returned to power.

So around the time when Jimmy made this speech the labour movement was active and fighting back, and of course at such times working people do not feel so alienated because they are participating in wider social activity; but unfortunately that period was brought to a long drawn out end when people's hopes and aspirations were muffled in Labour Governments which mislead and deserted the working people who had brought them to power. By the winter of 1978-79, later called the 'Winter of Discontent' the Labour Callaghan Government, which had abandoned the Keynesian full-employment economic policy brought in by the Attlee Government, was bogged down in a strike by low-paid Local Government workers fighting for a reasonable wage to live on.

We now know the outcome of that struggle, the workers got a wage increase, but the UK got Margaret Thatcher and full employment, plus decent wages and conditions for working people, took a tumble, as neo-liberal ideology strengthened its grip on the British people. Later In 1986 in her 'Big Bang' project for the city of London, Thatcher demolished much of the restrictions and regulations which controlled the Banking and Financial services and introduced to some extent the neo-liberal Financial Capitalism which now dominates the UK economy.

Financial Capitalism

Since the entrenchment of the neo-liberal ideology supported, and reinforced by the domination of financial capitalism our society in the UK. This ideology has expanded into other Western Countries, and has made a lurch to the right. Most people, not only workers, now find themselves trapped in an impersonal system which takes away from them any individual means of having an effective say in their daily affairs. The irony of this is that it is all done in the name of greater 'individual choice'.

We have all observed how having a wider range of choice for the consumer means closing small locally owned shops and directing everyone to supermarkets owned by large multi-national corporations. It means getting rid of nationally owned power and transport companies and having them run by multi-national companies. It means doing away with local Bank Managers who can make decisions about loans, and passing all this over to impersonal computers which deal directly with 'Head Office' of ever increasing super banks.

After all these years of making major changes to provide more customer choice, the ordinary customer is left with one choice, take it or leave it. We all now know there is no competition between the railway companies, the power companies, or the supermarkets. We are not fooled by the media advertising about changing your supplier, most people have sussed that this is all a big con, and that the big companies are working with each other against our interests.

They corner the market between them, and work as an oligopoly. They put pressure on local producers and drive down their living standards by flooding the market with imported goods from time to time, until in the end local producers are reduced and impoverished and the consumers are even more exposed to the Multi-national corporations.

This relentless drive towards the multi-national corporation super-state has, of course, different effect on different people, but we are all under its strong influence. Some try to join it and take part in the 'rat race.' For example some dairy farmers respond to the low milk prices by buying up and taking over their neighbour's farms cheaply and becoming large factory farms able to produce vast quantities at low unit cost. This option is of course limited to very few who have access to financial reserves. This means that for many local farmers there is no economic future for them and their families, however even for the successful few who survive they are now trapped in the 'rat race' because they now have a huge financial debt to service as well as their families and they are under the control of the same oligopoly who are still driving for lower prices, in order to get higher and quicker returns for their multi-national corporations.

So in this game, even the winners lose.

Since the multi-national corporations are backed by financial organisations, which have the power to make 'phantom' money, they are able to increasingly rig the 'free market' and keep it under their control. They also own and control the media (free Press) so they are able to buy and sell many politicians. This gives them political power in 'democratic' countries, without the difficulty of standing for election and justifying their objectives.

We all see it played out in front of us every day. Any politician who wants to challenge the establishment line, which is quite clear because it is carried by every news outlet, will be roundly condemned and under constant criticism. We will be told that he or she does not know what they are talking about and all sorts of well paid 'expert' will appear on the media to tell us how wrong and stupid this political figure is. They will advise us that such a politician is 'unelectable'. When this fails we will be told that the 'money markets' will reject his or her opinion and this will cause grave harm to our economy. Yet there is no such thing as 'money markets'. This concept, as we described in our book 'Moving On' has nothing to do with markets, it is merely the demands of financial organisations being expressed.

Anyone arriving on earth from another planet and examining our financial and political system would consider us mad to allow this system to dominate our economy and society. They might point out that the citizens of the UK are legally responsible for meeting the debts of sterling, but we do not control its supply, and we have to pay interest to private organisations if we want to use it. They would note that these private organisations ignore statutory regulations, openly ignore the law and make profits for themselves, while allowing the banking system to become bankrupt. That instead of treating such people as criminals we paid off their debts and allowed them to carry on operating 'Zombie' banks creating more 'phantom' money just as before, which again we will have to bail out in future. We appear to have no control, or say in the matter.

As Jimmy Reid pointed out in relation to these international corporations "The facts are there for all who want to see. Giant monopoly companies and consortia dominate almost every branch of our economy. – Government by the people for the people becomes meaningless unless it includes major economic decision making by the people for the people." Jimmy tells us this is not simply an economic issue, it is, he claims "In essence an ethical and moral question for whoever takes the important economic decisions in society, ipso facto determines the social priorities of that society."

Now the ordinary person in Scotland sees all of this, they are not unaware of these issues, they may not be able to articulate how this corruption actually works, but they know it is corruption. They see the politicians unable to even acknowledge this problem, while committing themselves and others to 'austerity' in order to meet the cost of this corruption.

This is the reason why alienation has grown a pace since Jimmy Reid's speech, the extension of financial capitalism places people in a position where they have less and less control of their lives and are increasingly becoming alienated and isolated, powerless and impotent in the world around them.

In response to this many people have just given up, they no longer see political democracy as being helpful, "all politicians are the same, they are all looking after their own interests" They might tell you, and on the surface this looks to be correct. Labour politicians change places with Tory politicians and we can't tell the difference. Both insist that we must support the bankers who run our economy, our media, and it would appear our political structures as well.

Finally, in the referendum campaign people saw the possibility that things could change. They saw all the traditional politicians, all the media, the BBC and the entire Establishment on the same side, against Scottish Independence, and they knew instinctively that the system was being challenged in a real sense, rather than the sham political pantomime of the Westminster show.

This was what created the huge 'grass roots' of the independence movement, which was in fact the very essence of the movement. Had this not developed and the Yes campaign been in the hands of the official Yes Campaign professionals, then it would have made little progress and would have fizzled out. The Yes Campaign was brought to life by the grass roots and this development in turn gave hope and power back to people who had lost all concept of what power they had, or could have.

This is what is at the very heart of the political movement which the referendum gave life and spirit to. The spark which ignited this movement and which will continue to motivate it is hope and the force that will drive it is people rejecting the alienation mantle which has been covering them and seeking involvement and a place in the new Scotland.

If we understand that, we will have picked up the message Jimmy Reid was drawing to our attention and we will be able to move forward with this mass movement to a better Scotland. We must however be quite clear about the nature of the new Scotland we want and about the obstacles in our path to obtain it. If we fully understand this, we have a duty to spread that understanding to the movement as a whole. Once the people have a good grasp of the issue, there will be nothing to stop the movement for independence and for a major change in our economy.

Media Influence.

It would be very foolish of us to move towards another referendum on Scottish Independence without looking carefully at the role the media played in the last one. Because this is a vital aspect of the democratic process, anyone who is interested in democracy has to recognise that in order to win people to your particular cause you need, first of all, the means of presenting your cause to them.

The Yes Campaign did not have that to any significant degree in the official media, the newspapers, radio and TV, and this weakness was shown to be a very serious disadvantage. It is true that in view of the significant support the Yes Campaign had among the young and among highly motivated educated people, this did give them an advantage in the social media.

Indeed the way the 'official' media reacted to this social media voice for the Yes Campaign demonstrates just how important they considered media cover to be in the referendum campaign. Unionist Politicians with the full backing of the Newspapers, Radio and TV mounted frequent and virulent attacks on the 'Cyber-Nats' they accused them of every sort of disgraceful behaviour known to man in their attempt to silence this media voice which they did not control.

The media, and Unionist politicians understood the importance of good regular supportive encouragement such as the media can provide to any campaign, those of us in the Yes Campaign were less aware of this, and we were very wrong. We should have recognised that their 'over the top' reaction to Yes Campaign support on social media was because of their recognition of how important it was while many of us failed to see that. We were too complacent about what we thought was the obvious weakness of the opposition's case in the media.

I realised, late in the day, when I was canvassing round the doors just before the referendum and speaking to many elderly voters that they were not much aware of the issues that had been debated on the social media. Many of them did not use it at all and those who did used it much less frequently than younger voters. It struck me that a very large section of the community did not get much information from social media, but they all had a TV pumping out propaganda in their living room every day.

Now if we look at what the 'neutral' BBC was pumping out, never mind the 'opposition' channels, you can see, certainly in hindsight, how many lies, distortions, omissions, misrepresentations, and errors they managed to make on that subject in the pre-referendum period. It is so vast it is not possible to address it to any great extent in this wee book. In this regard the research by Dr John Robertson of the University of West Scotland* into the BBC which identified considerable bias is worth consideration. Also GA Ponsonby's 'London Calling'* is a book which clearly illustrates this issue. If however we just confine ourselves to the very significant issues we may be able to see the pattern.

Let's take the positions adopted by David Cameron, the UK Prime Minister, and how they were reported in the media. In the early days of the movement towards a referendum, when it was widely predicted in the polls that in a straight Yes –No vote, the No vote would win significantly, David Cameron made it clear that he was totally opposed to 'Devo Max' as an option in the Independence Referendum.

He described 'Devo Max' as just a ploy by Alex Salmond to save face when he lost the referendum. David Cameron, with the full backing of the Labour and Liberal Parties was totally opposed to more devolution being considered in the referendum, what they wanted, he insisted, was that there should be a straight choice between the status quo and independence. The Labour and Lib/Dem leadership agreed with this and the media reported this giving it their sympathetic support.

When David Cameron met Alex Salmond to deliver this message, the media gave an extensive report on this explaining how Alex Salmond's trickery had been exposed by the Prime Minister's skill and he, and all the other party leaders were delighted with how he had exposed Salmond.

Later, when David Cameron signed the Edinburgh Agreement with Alex Salmond this principle was enshrined in it. i.e. that the referendum would be about a straight vote for or against independence with further devolution of any sort not being a part of the referendum. This agreement was later enacted into law confirming these arrangements and prohibiting both Governments from introducing new material during the election 'purdah' period.

However, we all now know what actually happened. Within the last week of the polling campaign, and after the postal ballot had been open for some time, the Westminster Government, and all the Unionist Party leaders dramatically changed their minds and wanted to offer 'Devo Max' to the Scottish electorate, and a Scottish newspaper printed the infamous 'Vow' on its front page, while the rest of the media went viral with reports on the new range of offers to Scots if they rejected independence.

In spite of the fact that it was now 'illegal' for the Westminster Government to make offers on devolution in order to influence the vote, Cameron ignored the Law and did this, supported by the other Unionist Party Leaders and by a well known Labour back-bencher called Gordon Brown, (now reportedly working for an American Finance Company).

Now the BBC, and the rest of the media, found nothing wrong with this sudden u-turn and breach of election law, on the contrary they gave it extensive and supportive coverage. What we now know is that in addition to the published opinion poll which predicted a narrow 2 point Yes lead; there was, more significantly, an unpublished more extensive Westminster Government poll, which, we now understand, gave the Yes Campaign a 10 point lead. This poll although paid for by the people was kept secret from them and has remained secret.

This breach of election law by the PM was not an isolated item, he did it consistently, and he used his office to lobby foreign Governments, even the Russian Government who told the world about it, asking them to comment against Scottish Independence. He briefed major companies asking them to make statements against Scottish Independence. He also acted contrary to Company Law as well by encouraging leaks from RBS all geared to this same objective and he involved the civil service in this activity. All of this was in breach of electoral law, and undermined the democratic process. In all of this, he had the unfailing support of the neutral BBC and of course the rest of the media. Nothing could have been more undemocratic than this exercise, but he wasn't finished yet.

In a BBC interview on the 17th of September 2014 David Cameron was asked specifically by Laura Kuenssberg if extra powers being promised to the Scottish Parliament might not lead to demands for more powers of English members of Parliament. His response was that the situation was not remotely at that stage yet. Two days later, on the 19th of September he called a news conference outside Number 10 to announce his plan for English Votes for English Laws (EVEL). This was a cynical disrespect for the Scottish electorate, but this was not challenged by the media.

Postal Ballot Rigging

Finally the PM, perhaps in desperation, carried out one other undemocratic move which has been hidden ever since and which the media has made no attempt to examine. The Postal Ballot in the Independence Referendum was rigged. Anyone who gives this matter serious consideration can't fail to see this, and it is clear that this was not done by amateurs. The Postal Ballot was interfered with not in a crude way, but by reading Local Government confidential computers. This could not have been done by any political party, but it could have been done by MI5. If MI5 did this rigging, then David Cameron must have sanctioned it.

Now of course there will be outrage at this suggestion. How dare I, or anyone else, suggest that such a thing could happen? The only defence I have, my only excuse against this torrent of outrage which could come from the media is that all the facts point me in that direction and as Burns told us "facts are cheils that winna ding". There are a number of disturbing facts about the Postal Ballot in the Scottish referendum which I just can't put to rest, and which the media is not interested in. If you, or the media think you have a reasonable explanation for them perhaps you could make them public. In the meantime, since I know that MI5 would have the means of rigging this ballot in the particular way in which it appears to have been rigged, It seems to be the most rational explanation. Here are my disturbing facts:

(a)   The extremely high PV turnouts (96.4% in one area) which were not widely reported.

(b)   The co-relation between the PV and the No vote as demonstrated in the DSF report*. And

(c)   The fact that several people including, John McTernan and Ruth Davidson, reported on the outcome of this postal ballot before the vote was counted.

None of these questions have been resolved in spite of a police inquiry into a public claim that Tory party supporters in Scotland had been involved in blatant breaches of Scottish law.

This shocking report came from a strange source, from the leader of the Scottish Tory party, no less, one Ruth Davidson MSP. She publicly announced this criminal activity on BBC TV to the population of Scotland in general, although she claimed not to know it was criminal.

You could not 'make it up' could you? Ruth Davidson, leader of the Scottish Tories, claimed on TV to know the result of the Postal Ballot in the Scottish Referendum before the sealed election boxes were opened. She then 'explained' having such knowledge to Tory party supporters blatantly breaking the law, and this led to a police investigation.

The police of course found no evidence of this alleged offence after interviewing Ruth Davidson twice, which is hardly surprising, because her explanation is very hard to accept. It requires a large number of people, including Local Government Officers to be involved in illegal activity, which is not really credible.

However the important question remains, how did Ruth Davison get this information? It could not have been obtained by legal means. She is telling us all to put the referendum behind us and move on, so she can help in this respect by telling us where she got the information about the contents of the Postal Ballot boxes.

Her false claim about Tory supporters being involved in criminal activity was an attempt to explain how she had such knowledge, correct knowledge as it turned out to be, of the contents of official sealed ballot boxes before they were opened at the count. However the police found her claim to have no substance.

Had her claim been true, such people would have been involved in criminal activity for which they could have been sentenced to a two year prison term. I'm not surprised that the police found this not to have any substance. The question remains however, where did Ruth Davidson get this information? She appeared on the TV on the night of the referendum confident and bubbling with excitement, about the Postal Ballot which had not been counted at that time, yet she could not contain her delight with the result from the Postal Ballot, but how did she know what it contained?

Indeed how did John McTernan know four days before that, what was in the Postal Ballot? Was it all down to his skill as a 'political expert''? Let's look at John McTernan's remarkable ability, not only to predict the outcome of the postal ballot, but to predict its higher per-cent age turnout from the poll-stations turnout, fairly accurately, and to predict its overall effect on the outcome of the ballot, all before the boxes were opened.

Now John McTernan is an 'expert' in political judgement no doubt, he has been paid a salary by the Labour party to give advice on his political foresight so it must be assumed that he has a particular gift at this: On the other hand he predicted that Labour in Scotland would retain all its MPs at the 2015 GE, indeed that it may increase its number. Not a very accurate prediction. His predictions about Jeremy Corbyn's leadership race result were somewhat out also, as was his prediction of the recent Oldham by-election, so perhaps his judgement on these things is not as sharp as he advertises.

Yet he was spot-on on his claims about the Postal Ballot, how did he manage that? Well he will have had contacts with MI5 from his days working for Blair at number 10. Again I have no idea about these matters I just allow the facts that I do have to direct me towards possible explanations. What I do know however without a shadow of a doubt, is that the UK media are not at all interested in these strange facts which are so disturbing to me.

It is now clear to me that a number of studies in the UK and in Europe* have shown that the UK Postal Ballot system is wide open to abuse. I was not aware of this, and I suppose most people in Scotland are not aware of it either, but I'm sure the media are.

Before there is any other important ballot in Scotland we must get this Postal Ballot system put right. The policy seems to be that convenience is what it most important about ballot arrangements; this is nonsense. What is paramount about ballots is that they are secure and that the result is honest and trustworthy, and if we have to sacrifice some voter convenience for that it is in a good cause. What we can't allow is for the current UK Postal Ballot system with all its weaknesses to be used to such a wide extend in Scotland again, and certainly not in an independence referendum.

Reasons for an Independence Referendum.

Nicola Sturgeon, our First Minister, wisely did not attempt to define all the reasons which would lead the Scottish people to determine that another independence referendum should be held, although she gave some possible examples. From my own perspective I do not accept that Scotland ever had the Independence Referendum which was agreed between the Scottish Government and the UK Government in the Edinburgh Agreement.

As I have indicated this agreement was abused by the UK Government right from the start, it treated with entire disrespect the legal framework which it had itself agreed and the whole process was undemocratic. So if we have a democratic referendum on Scottish independence sometime in the future it will be the first proper one we have had. So one good reason for having a democratic referendum on this issue is because we tried to arrange this before and the whole process was flawed.

However, moving on, there are many reasons why Scottish people should now want to hold a democratic referendum. Like Nicola, I would not attempt to try to define each of these reasons, but one of them stands out like a sore thumb. If the Scottish economy is being strangled and prevented from functioning in a manner which would best meet the needs of the Scottish people, this would be an obvious reason why the Scottish people might decide to have a referendum on independence.

I believe that this book identifies the fact that the Scottish banking system needs significant reform if it is to meet the needs of the Scottish economy. If this fact becomes evident to the people as a whole then they will demand that it is addressed. If this were attempted it would soon be obvious that only an Independent Scotland could do this.

Another area worthy of our attention is the situation in relation to renewable energy. The Scottish Government has embraced this new technology and its economic implications in a significant way. Indeed Scotland is being recognised internationally as one of the leading nations in the struggle to combat climate change. Our efforts however are being undermined by the attitude of the UK Government, which appears to be sabotaging our effort in this regard wherever they can.

On the issue of human rights once again we have the UK Government attempting to move against international consensus and against existing Legal Provision, or in the case of the anti-trade-union legislation, introducing legislation against people's rights. It should be clear to all that trade-union rights are, as Jimmy Reid claimed, 'human rights'. In this area the First Minister told an STUC Rally in Glasgow,* The Scottish Government would not be forced by Westminster legislation to employ agency labour to 'break' strikes, or to refuse to provide check-off facilities for trade unions or engage in hostile actions against trade-unions. This of course under our current constitutional arrangements in the UK would be in breach of the law. However as we have seen the UK Political establishment did not hesitate to break the law when this suited their interests, they broke the purdah conditions in the Independence Referendum in blatant breach of the law.

If we are being faced with conflicts in the legislation coming out of Westminster, legislation which has no democratic mandate in Scotland, and the fundamental interests of Scottish people's economic or human rights are being challenged; then there is no question about it this could trigger the decision by the Scottish people to have a referendum. The Scottish people must however ensure that in the arrangements for any referendum in future, every effort is made to avoid the mistakes of the last time, and learn the lessons also.

The main lesson to be learned is to recognise, from the start, that while there may be a small official steering group to direct the Yes Campaign, the real campaign however will be an extensive mass movement rooted in communities and involving people from all political parties and none.

This lesson must be remembered. We must ensure that the new Yes Campaign from the very start embraces all sections of our diverse modern Scottish community, and like last time gives a place and a voice to all these various groups.

Any new Referendum Campaign must once again be an open invitation for the sovereign Scottish people to demonstrate their power and their nobility and we must ensure that their voice and opinions are widely available to all the people. We must demand our own BBC TV time to control and produce our own news programmes to ensure that the Yes Campaign message gets into every household.

* Gordon Macintyre-Kemp "the National" Friday 18th December 2015.

* Jimmy Reid 'Rectorial address' Glasgow University 28th April 1972.

* Dr John Robertson, Reader in Media Politics, University West of Scotland. February 2014.

* G A Ponsonby 'London Calling' How the BBC stole the Referendum.

* DSF 'Defending Democracy' Report Dunoon 2015.

* The Telegraph "Postal voting fraud is easy, Electoral Commissioner says" Tower Hamlets case.

* STUC Rally Glasgow Concert Halls 10th December 2015.

—ww—

I have tried to make this book as readable as possible to the widest audience and have therefore not given the extensive appendices and an index as we did in the book 'Moving On'. I have identified my sources for of the main points I make at the end of each chapter so that these can be easily checked by any who wish to do so.

This book is in a sense a step on from the book 'Moving On' and should be read as such. It addresses the same issues, but where 'Moving On' identified the economic and financial situation which an independent Scotland required; 'Currency – In an Independent Scotland' identifies who we can get there.

Andy Anderson